businessplan.com

how to write an eCommerce business plan

Second Edition

l. manning ross

OASIS PRESS BOOKS & SOFTWARE

THE OASIS PRESS®
CENTRAL POINT, OREGON

Published by The Oasis Press®/PSI Research
© 1998, 2000 by L. Manning Ross

This publication is designed to provide accurate and authoritative information in regard to the subject matter covered. It is sold with the understanding that the author and publisher are not engaged in rendering legal, accounting, or other professional service. If legal advice or other expert assistance is required, the services of a competent professional person should be sought.

— from a declaration of principles jointly adopted by a committee of the American Bar Association and a committee of publishers.

Interior design by Eliot House Productions
Cover design by Steven Burns

Please direct any comments, questions, or suggestions regarding this book to:

The Oasis Press®/PSI Research
Editorial Department
P.O. Box 3727
Central Point, Oregon 97502-0032

(541) 245-6502
(541) 245-6505 fax
info@psi-research.com email

The Oasis Press® is a Registered Trademark of Publishing Services, Inc., an Oregon corporation doing business as PSI Research.

Visit the author's website at *http://www.lmanning-ross.com*

Library of Congress Cataloging-in-Publication Data

Ross, L. Manning (Lynn Manning), 1945 –
    Businessplan.com: how to write an ecommerce business plan / L. Manning Ross. — 2nd ed.
        p.   cm. — (PSI successful business library)
    Includes index.
    ISBN 1-55571-531-1 (paper)
        1. Business planning.   2. Business enterprises — Computer networks — Management. 3.
Internet (Computer network) 4. World Wide Web. I. Series

HD30.28.R664   2000
658.4'012—dc21   00-035621

Printed and bound in the United States of America
Second Edition 10 9 8 7 6 5 4 3 2 1

 Printed on recycled paper when available.

Contents

The Author

Lynn Manning Ross, business technologist turned author, has been help-ing companies for over 22 years achieve success through strategic planning, technology utilization and more recently, eCommerce. *businessplan.com* cap-tures this practical, hands-on experience gleaned from working with nearly 800 clients globally, and shows readers step-by-step how to write an eCommerce business plan.

eCommerce
Technology Adoption Issues
Executive Coach
Management Consultant

Lynn Manning Ross

www.lmanning-ross.com
sponsored by: yahoo.com

P.O. Box 12292
La Jolla, California 92039-2292
lmr@lmanning-ross.com
619-209-2797

Acknowledgments

To Many Talented Professionals, Thank You

In alphabetical order:

Sonia Alvarado, Karen Axelton, Scott Banister, Don B. Bradley III, Gary Brooks, Munira Brooks, Rebecca Brown, Todd Buranen, Steven E. Burns, Kathleen Cahill, John Cook, Kathleen W. Corbin, Donna Cotton, Tracy J. Crowe, Rachael Farber, Bob Gaertner, Carlo Di Giovanni, Rami Hadar, Tresea Hays, Lance Hoffman, Heidi S. Hooper, Eric P. Hvolboll, Lorna Keith, Paul Kephart, Michael Killen, Christine Kim, Daniel Koch, Bob Kreutter, Richard Leavitt, Sharon LeBlanc, Chuck Locurto, Chris Lucas, John J. McGrath, Harris N. Miller, Stephen J. Mihalic, Judith Van Noate, Juliette Noh, Alexander F. Obbard, Adelina Ortega, Hugh O'Brian, Sharon J. O'Shea, Mark Palaske, Patrick Parsche, Jack Pellerin, Kenneth J. Pontifex, Patty Poston, Rick Reiman, Rhonda Revercomb, Catherine Louise Rischard, Perry N. Ritenour, Russ Robinson, Lisa Rossi, Amy Serrill, Judith L. Sigsworth, Kimberly Stubbs, John W. Sunnen, William S. "Tom" Thomas, Jr., Julie A. Thompson, John Trelle, Robert G. Voorhees, Jeff Walsh, Jeanie M. Welch, Pamela A. White, David M. White.

Preface

"The overland mail stages are soon to pass this way. Our road is nearly complete too. It would be fine for us to have an opportunity of sending letters twice a week."

– Judge Charles Fernald, February 20, 1861
founder of California's first law firm

Unknown a few short years ago, the Internet hit the world center stage bringing with it a radical paradigm shift in the way we conduct business and communicate. Industry experts are now predicting a global growth of over $1.17 trillion in combined sales by year's end 2002. *businessplan.com* was written to help you catch this wave of opportunity by mixing faithful strategic planning procedures with the latest Web technology to produce an eCommerce business plan.

Just imagine a business arena where customers worldwide are greeted by name, where you can identify, interact, and track individual customers and prime prospects instantly. Or just imagine holding a meeting in virtual space with colleagues working from five locations around the globe. You are discussing the elements of structural design and all six of you visit the proposed building together, at the same time, from your own offices thousands of miles apart.

You inspect the building inside and out, discuss changes, make decisions, identify suppliers and conclude your meeting. There is no travel, no per diem, no tips, downtime or expense reports. The project was identified, bid, accepted, coordinated, developed, and staffed with experts from around the world in cyberspace. Will it become a tangible building on a plot of earth with a street address? Yes.

This is now. This is the future. This is how technology is shaping and will continue to shape lifestyles, the nature of jobs, organizations, costs, our customers, clients, supply chain, distribution channels, marketing, sales, and most importantly, business planning. It is fresh, innovative, global, instant, and profitable.

– Lynn Manning Ross
www.lmanning-ross.com

Ah! eCommerce

What You Need to Know about eCommerce is Available at any Grocery Check Out Counter

At the turn of the last millennium, no one could have imagined the impact eCommerce would have on the way we do business. And we haven't even begun! It is no longer a question of wait and see. It's now a question of how do we do it? As Aneurin Bosley, Editor-in-Chief, *The Internet Business Journal*, predicted with such accuracy in late 1993, "The Internet is the basis of a paradigm shift in the structure of regional and global economic systems."

What is eCommerce anyway? Associated with the Web, eCommerce simply means *doing business electronically*. More accurately, it is a technical process that collapses the transactional timeline between communicating parties. For example, using a fax machine is also a device for doing business electronically. Prompted by the popularity of the Internet though, eCommerce has become the catchword for conducting business over the Web. But as a technical process, eCommerce has nothing to do with creating graphically pleasing Web pages, although it is that too.

The irony is almost everything one needs to know about eCommerce is available at any grocery check out counter! The next time you buy groceries take a close look at the receipt. Chances are it looks like the example on the following page.

Information from this sales receipt, when combined with thousands of sales receipt data, becomes a blue print for operating and managing the grocery market. In fact, nearly every company collects similar data about their customers whether it sells business-to-consumer or business-to-business. Information technology (IT) has become so sophisticated that combinations of data are almost limitless, privacy issues notwithstanding.

In this instance, the grocery market will develop a database to compare and analyze each of the pieces of information shown on the receipt. The customer profile alone will produce combinations of data helping corporate executives as well as store managers make informed decisions as to how they should operate their company or plan promotional campaigns. One example is the customer's product preferences and buying frequency.

When these data are combined with other customer preference data from the sales receipts, the pattern will clearly show the total number of customers within a

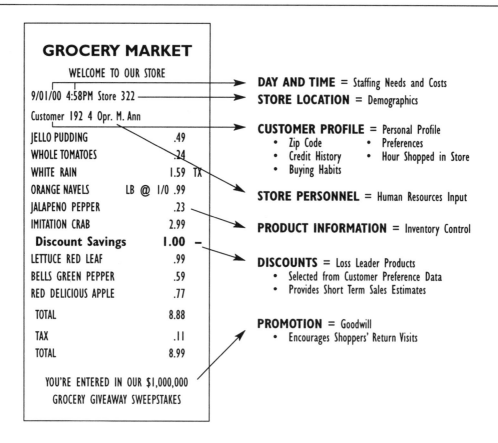

marketing area, the different types of products they prefer and how often they buy these items. Grocery executives know that boosting weekly sales becomes a matter of choosing and promoting these designated "specials," or loss leaders, in the legendary Thursday section of the local newspaper.

eCommerce is similar. eCompanies need and utilize the same type of data when they conduct eBusiness. The difference is all data collection and transactional communication is completed over the Internet electronically versus from a physical location such as the grocery market. The advantages are obvious whether the company is a retailer expanding its marketing reach through e-tailing or strictly a virtual business void of any brick-and-mortar.

In the grocery receipt analogy payment is made in person. On an eCommerce website money is transferred electronically. Tracking customers or visitors to a website is equivalent to recording the day, time, store location and customer profile. Capturing customer preferences and buying habits on a website are equal to brick-and-mortar product mix and inventory control. This includes services as well. Promotions, of course, are a universal part of doing business on or off the Internet.

Decisions for opening a virtual company are done in the same way as they are in a traditional business. For instance, if you were opening a retail store, starting a service business or buying a franchise there are literally hundreds of details to consider. The same analogy holds true for expanding a company. You're not expected to be adept in every facet of the start-up or expansion process. You hire the required talent — from the painter to an attorney.

Some of the first questions these experts will ask are, "What do you plan to do?" "How many rooms (or square feet) are there?" "What about signage?" "What colors do you have in mind?" "What is your budget?" "Are we talking about growing a colossal empire or a little cottage business?" And so on.

Errrrr, uh, hmmm answers delay accomplishments. If you are not sure what you want, no one else will be either. If you have written a business plan, answers come easily. Colossal business ideas are approached one way; cottage-size ones another.

Writing a plan is even more important today than in the past. Jennifer James, six-time author and urban cultural anthropologist said it best, "We are changing faster than any previous generation. The changes are rapid, deep, and broad. Technology generates the speed, economics drives the breadth, and cultural shifts create the depth. We are being forced not just to change our way of thinking and working but our ways of living and feeling. Become aware of the new forms of intelligence necessary for the future and the skills that generate a 21st century mind."

These "new forms of intelligence" are forcing us to rethink every aspect of managing a company from the bottom up and top down as we weave our markets around the globe. businessplan.com was written with a strong sense for helping you gain a better understanding of this new business model, the decision making process and then articulate these decisions in your business plan using the sample text and worksheets that are provided in this book.

The eBasics that follow are meant as over simplified summaries for the main aspects of doing business over the Internet. Becoming an expert isn't necessary. Becoming conversant is extremely helpful. For an in-depth evaluation of these and other topics, there are an abundance of self-study books, articles, and classes as well as white papers for every technology-related subject.

eBasics

Obviously, the Web is rapidly hitting critical mass. Just walk by any well stocked magazine stand, listen to the nightly news or watch any commercial — dot-com has invaded us, not only in English but in every other prominent language in the world. On the surface, it's easy to be left with the impression that the whole world knows more about running a virtual company than say — you. Although that is highly unlikely, the following eBasics will speed up your learning curve.

Bandwidth

Bandwidth is available in many sizes ranging from the width of a, so called, sidewalk to more than a 20 lane freeway. If bandwidth were lines on a page the different widths might look something like the following comparison in Example 1 on page 4.

EXAMPLE 1 (not to scale)

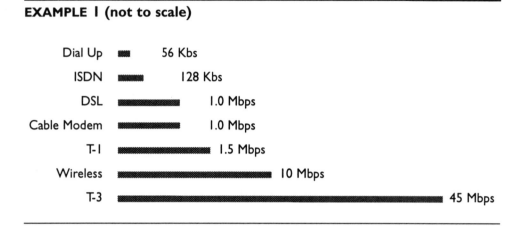

The type of connection needed depends upon what a company constantly transmits over the Internet. The size of the business can be deceiving having little to do with their bandwidth requirement. A graphic designer with a home-based business needs greater bandwidth to transmit graphic content over the Internet than a 10 person legal firm that primarily transmits text documents. Corporate giants usually have T-3 lines. Small- and mid-sized businesses fall somewhere in between.

Computer Capacity

Equate the capacity of your computers to commercial space. Does your business require 500 square feet or 50,000? How much Internet traffic is anticipated? How many internal or external users? A very small business with a 50-page catalog displaying 300 products will need a much larger hard drive capacity than a predominately text based company such as a research firm. Graphics hog space not only on a computer but on websites as well. Use the following approximations as a guide:

1 Megabyte (MB) = 80 pages of text
1 GIG = 1,000 MB or 80,000 pages of text

Other options include having a Web hosting company or ISP house your site on their servers versus housing your own site. It is a lot less expensive allowing you to start small and rent more capacity as you grow. There are other advantages as well. Most all Internet utility companies offer an assortment of eCommerce solutions such as shopping carts, merchant's accounts or database services. You pay for what you use versus investing in the software, expensive servers, and managing the site.

Consider this, too, if you house your own site there is a possibility that it might be out of service from too much success! Remember when eBay's computers crashed under the heavy traffic load? "Prevention is worth a pound of cure," especially when it comes to technology.

Just like the grocery market that tracks its customer volume hourly, you need to do the same thing or at least estimate the amount of traffic. It isn't sufficient to think in terms of 24-hour cycles because the traffic flow is constantly changing just like it does on real world freeways. Say you have 24,000 site visitors per a 24-hour period. If you estimate that this number of visitors represents 1,000 visitors per hour and buy a server to handle, say, 2,000 visitors per hour thinking your computer capacity is more than enough, you may be out of luck. What if 16,000 of these visitors hit your site within a four-hour period? There are other sporadic traffic periods that will occur too. What about timed advertising, public relation activities, sales campaigns, links to affiliate sites, and inevitable company growth? Here is a quick checklist to help you make sure your server has sufficient muscle to handle your website and keep it in business.

- Java, JavaScript and flashy graphics slow down how your Web pages load on the visitor's computer. This, alone, will consume bandwidth while too many people are all trying to download pages and do business with you at the same time. Think of an over crowded restaurant where the majority of diners linger far too long. The restaurant makes money from filling up and emptying its tables so many times during peak dinning periods. When diners linger beyond an acceptable time, the restaurant loses money. The same analogy is true on your site. Design the site so it is fast to download. Users quickly get what they need and leave. Just like in the restaurant, this releases their spot to someone else.
- If you plan on doing business globally, think about mirroring your site with an overseas ISP. It is also a plus to have a native speaking Web host help you with the foreign language philology after the site copy has been carefully translated.
- Add more RAM than you think you will ever need.
- Review server logs daily. Slim down or turn off the processes you seldom use or don't need.

Domain Name Registration

Whether you already have a website URL (universal resource locator) or URI (universal resource indicator), need one or want to acquire another, the quickest way to obtain a name is to connect to the central resource for registering Internet names *www.networksolutions.com*. A search engine on their home page makes it fast and easy to find out if the name you want is available. Once a name is selected, simply follow the directions for registering it. The company offers payment options including paying by credit card. If the name you want isn't available, go to *www.neologist.com* to see who owns the domain and other pertinent information. The name might be for sale.

Incidentally, if you are new to the Web, an URL or URI are the equivalent of a unique telephone number and how people find your website. All URL's begin with http:// even though it isn't always necessary to type it in when calling up a site. Early entrants on the Web used "www" following the http:// such as http://www. That, too, isn't always necessary for retrieving a site. The URI is a "work in progress" from Tim Berners-Lee, sometimes referred to as the father of the Web.

Email

Turning the Web into an eCommerce tool begins in the early planning stages. A good starting place is to recognize doing business on the Internet begins and ends with your capability to interact with others via email.

Both email addresses and website URL's distinguish between user types and always include the now famous dot — like the period before .com as shown in the following list. Excluding .com and .net, the current list is as old as the Net itself. Growth, however, has prompted Internet planners to consider other handles. Since most for-profit enterprises use .com or .net, it is impossible to tell if a personalized email address or website is the alias of a giant corporation or a business of one, an obvious advantage for smaller companies.

Current		Planned	
.com	commercial	.arts	arts & cultural groups
.edu	educational – 4 year	.firm	firms
.gov	government – U.S.	.info	information services
.mil	military	.nom	personal sites
.net	network infrastructure	.rec	recreational
.org	organization	.store	merchandise sales
		.web	emphasizing the Web

Elementary but worth repeating for those starting out, email addresses are distinguished from URL's by the @ sign dividing the name of a sender from its URL. For example, *marysmith@nytec.com*. The name "nytec" is the company's personalized URL. The .com indicates the type of enterprise. An email address may be written either, Mary Smith *<marysmith@nytec.com>* or *marysmith@nytec.com*. The difference is adding the name Mary Smith before the address, in which case the brackets on either side of the email address are used to set off its destination.

The kind of email software you choose and the type of Internet Service Provider (ISP) depends upon the complexities of the company. For instance, does your business involve a lot of travel? If so, seek an ISP that offers a permanent email address that can be accessed from a website anywhere in the world. This is one way it works.

You are sitting in your customer's guest office in another city or half way around the world and want to download your email or send email. Simply access the Web as you normally do from your host's computer, type in your ISP's website URL and follow the directions from their home page. It is usually easy to do and a just few clicks to your private mail box. This is one of many ways any employee or business can connect to customers, colleagues and associates worldwide via an ISP's website.

There are any number of email software packages. Some will work better than others for your organization including those found in programs like Eudora Lite, Eudora Pro, Lotus Notes, Outlook and Netscape. Again your email investment depends upon what your company really needs. Overkill is expensive — another good reason for developing an eCommerce business plan. Then there is priority email.

Priority Email! It's all priority, delivered in seconds. Well yes, but ordinary email is not scanned for viruses. Email can also be registered where security is required for critical documents, such as legal papers or human resources and traced point-to-point. Fabrik Communications *www.fabrik.com* was the first to offer this service. The company has an off-site processing center where messages are scanned for viruses and then routed within a virtual private network (VPN) for about the same price as postage. The investment in the service is minimal since your existing software and hardware can be used. The U.S. Post Office is proposing a similar service.

Intranets

Equal to the importance of email is a company's Intranet — the internal Web pages not shared with the public. Intranet content includes, but is not limited to, information used by employees who work on projects together, marketing data, sales activities, the corporate research library and human resources, such as posting the company's Policies and Procedures Manual. Intranets simplify how information is distributed and managed throughout the organization. More over, it can reduce associated operating costs per employee between 65 to 95 percent over a 12-month period.

If your Intranet is extensive, and this has nothing to do with the size of your company, a search engine can easily be added. If you have used the Web you don't need an explanation, but if not, a search capability on the website itself will let users type in a few key words describing what they want. Users then click on the command word "go" or "search" and/or hit the enter key on their computer keyboards. That's it. The information is delivered to the user's computer screen.

Customer Conveniences

Whether your eCompany employs one or thousands, many functions are quite similar. For instance, an industrial design service might choose to give customers a personalized pin number. This would allow customers to access a designated area of its Intranet so they could review their design projects, make changes if needed and then place an order — all from the convenience of the customer's office. Again, the size of the company has absolutely nothing to do with this type of innovation and customer convenience. It is an eCommerce solution that will add yet another effective way to reach, sell and service customers.

There are many innovative ideas for helping customers do eBusiness with you. Pricing isn't always the end-all solution to competition. Customer service is. Make it convenient, easy, and fast for customers to find what they need or want, contact you, make purchases, and then exit your website.

The buzz on the Web is the need for Customer Service Resource (CSR) centers. A new twist to the common 800 number, these centers have living people answering customer questions in real-time voice and email over the Internet. Many companies are developing their own Web CSR's. Many other companies are offering CSR services to smaller companies for very reasonable fees.

CSR's, like 800 numbers, have already proven that personal interaction increases website sales and improves customer relations. It seems ironic, in too many instances, the same decision makers who recognize the need for CSR's are the same ones who employ non-personal anti-communication tactics.

You know these decision makers all too well. They are the ones who use voice mail as a gatekeeper, not only on their own phones but also allow the practice throughout the organization — including the sales department! They also endorse the anti-business practice of not returning regular business phone calls in a timely manner or fail to see the relevance of providing phone numbers on websites and other print media. Maybe the success of CSR centers is a wake up call for revisiting forgotten business protocol where human contact is seen as being equal to speed.

As millions more websites explode around the world, the competitive battle will be fought in the customer service department in real-time. While no one can deny that attracting customers through shrewd marketing tactics and stellar advertising campaigns is mandatory, building brand loyalty through superior customer services is master of the game.

Sales Tools

Efficiency notwithstanding, *effectively* using the Web for marketing and sales purposes needs to be at the forefront of every competitive decision. Scene: you need to make a large scale sales presentation that demonstrates your website. Problem? You discovered at the last minute that the meeting room is not set up for Internet connectivity. Scene: you need to discuss aspects of your company's website with the head buyer. Problem? The buyer's network is down and you can't return to her office for three weeks.

Meet a $49.95 solution called WebWhacker. Originally developed by ForeFront Direct *www.ffg.com* and now available from Blue Squirrel *www.bluesquirrel.com*, the WebWhacker lets you "whack" your site off the Web onto your laptop and go. Every megabyte is right there when you need it — every byte! You don't have to worry about being able to access the Internet. Plus your site can be viewed at highly accelerated speeds, a bonus for sales presentations.

WebCD, another excellent software package, combines a complete website with other sales media on a CD-ROM. Think how convenient it would be to take your entire website, training materials, product information, multimedia sales presentations, whole catalogs and so on, with you on a CD-ROM and set up for an instant replay anywhere, anytime for anyone. This is true mobility without having to be connected to the Internet. After the presentation, you can leave your CD-ROM with the prospect, investor, banker, customer or supplier. Developed by MarketScape *www.marketscape.com*, a company's entire sales department can travel in an executive's proverbial back pocket.

In addition to personal sales calls, a multitude of sales techniques abound on the Web. Affiliation programs are the most popular and one of the easiest to set up. All you have to do is identify the websites akin to your product or service and determine if they offer distribution or affiliation programs. Once on the site, click on the appropriate contact button. An online form will usually pop up. Fill it out and submit it.

When approved, you must agree to display their logo on your site and direct preselected product sales to them. Commissions vary from site to site. Although the cost is zero, there is an investment of time to set it up. If you don't maintain your own website, there are costs involved for hiring those who can post logos and create the links between sites. From time-to-time there will be some maintenance and revisions in either time or money or both.

A step up from affiliation programs is creating and owning your own Net storefront with help from your parent site such as Vstore or Affinia. Product is sold and commissions are made from your virtual store in much the same way as they are with an affiliation program. The difference is posting an affiliate's website logo with sales passing through your site to the affiliate's site where the order is filled to displaying the product on your website and having the sale pass through the parent to the original resource. There are variations, of course, with innovative ideas being introduced almost daily.

Marketing Research

Data collection, retrieval, and information management are what make the sales glitz work. Known as time consuming and expensive activities, many smaller companies forego serious marketing research. Thanks to the Internet times have changed. Commercial database companies are making it easy for anyone with a limited knowledge of data gathering to quickly become an expert.

For instance, somewhere, every day, marketing departments are forming composite pictures of how to position their product line to gain a larger market share both on and offline; an investor is questioning her next venture; an entrepreneur is wondering if the market surrounding his proposed toy store will support it. And what about *www.toys.com*? How will this eCompany affect brick-and-mortar toy sales on Main Street?

Who are my competitors? Where should I locate my business? What kind of inventory should we carry? What zip codes should we target? Does this investment live up to that one? Is this eCommerce business plan too ambitious or not ambitious enough?

Finding answers is not too difficult; statistics abound worldwide. Libraries, universities, governments, city planners and others have been collecting and archiving information for years, and now nearly all of these data are available over the Internet. Unfortunately, not all data accessed over the Web are user-friendly, current or easy to find, until recently.

Case in point. It is midnight. You are in a hotel room preparing for an important meeting early tomorrow. In a flash, a new idea is born, but is there a market for it? The idea is worth exploring, at least on paper, and then you remember Claritas Connect *www.claritas.com*, a commercial database provider. Dialing from your laptop, you go online, reach Claritas and have instant access to 64+ million pieces of data.

With an easy point and click, you begin shopping around. You need a number of site studies, consumer expenditures and segmentation data. Reviewing the data and sample reports, you decide to look at a few other examples prior to requesting an automatic retrieval.

There isn't a lot of time if you want to be fresh for a 7:00 A.M. meeting. Now is a good time to let this online service produce these data as attractive printed reports. When added to several other pages you already have, a preliminary report will be ready for your meeting. The cost for this transaction is minimal; less than $10.

A lack of marketing research can bring a company to its knees. There is always the chance, too, that good business development dollars are chasing bad data output, and in turn, faulty marketing plans are developed. All too often, marketing managers gloss over the aphorism, "markets are completely recycled every 10 years." Data then, decreases in value by 10 percent for every year it is out of date. Trends change along with the data as well.

While marketing dollars are being allocated, they might not be targeted to hit the mark 100 percent of the time. To stay ahead of its projected growth curve, a company must allow for annual market churn as well as inflation in projecting its sales goals. Clean, current data can help do this. Of course, not every business needs detailed updated data on a continuing basis, but if you are among those who do, marketing database companies, such as Claritas can offer inexpensive solutions keyed to your industry.

Research-It *www.iTools.com/* is another website for finding a variety of reference tools. A quick one-stop search station, Research-It links to dictionaries, thesauruses, quotations, language translators and other pertinent business resources, such as geographic maps and facts. And for hard copy lovers, *The Industry Standard*, *www.thestandard.com*, is a must Internet industry magazine for any serious eBusiness reader.

Tracking Customers

Competing has never been easier — or more complex! You've written a solid eCommerce business plan and have a website. Now what? Remember the grocery receipt and its customer database. You can capture the same helpful data from site visitors in a number of ways. You can encourage visitors to freely give you information by having them register to use your site or capture buyer data when users make purchases. Another way is to use digital watermarking.

If you are not familiar with the technology, a digitally watermarked image retains smart content that is, it not only communicates your copyright and contact information, but it can also direct viewers back to your website for retrieving other product-related information. It is an easy way to create a one-to-one relationship with the customer — every marketer's dream. The technology can also be used to make certain co-branding partners are using the most current images and not outdated ones.

Another way to capture customer information is to provide a chat room, a long-time staple of the Internet. Your chat room can also serve many other purposes. It can deliver real-time customer service (see Customer Conveniences, on page 7), provide for project discussions among team members, help you understand and solve a buyer's problem as well as support internal training.

Websites

Software for developing websites is improving as rapidly as the Internet is expanding. Most people know by now that websites are written in HTML code or Hyper Text Markup Language and anything beyond one Web page must link to other pages within the site. You must also let users *freely* leave the site at will. Although some sites hold users prisoner; it's a bad idea.

Now there is a new kid on the block — XML. According to Sean McGrath, author of *XML by Example: Building eCommerce Applications* (Prentice-Hall Computer Books, 1998), "HTML lets you describe the way data looks. XML lets you say what data means. Smart data is what is powering the eCommerce revolution."

Developing an eCommerce site requires some programming skills to set up order forms, automatic responses, and the like — a time and labor intensive project. But this is rapidly changing too. For example, many website development applications cross the boarder into the next generation of tools by delivering many eCommerce capabilities.

Some of the popular website development software includes Fusion by NetObjects, Frontpage from Microsoft and the Java Commerce Toolkit from Sun Microsystems. Sun also has a number of "partnering" programs to help entrepreneurial companies overcome many of their customary start up problems. One of these programs, Internet Associates,™ cuts equipment costs as well as offering a "broad portfolio" of technical support, education and integration in 130 countries worldwide.

A program such as Internet Associates may seem like overkill for micro to mid-size companies, but it isn't. If you intend to manage a global company from a few keyboards, you need reliability on a global scale — perhaps not at first, but as you grow. eCommerce is definitely here to stay and this kind of groundwork buys you a secure seat in the future.

One more brief word about websites, use daily backup tapes if the site is maintained in-house. If it is maintained on another server or with an ISP, tape backup should be part of the service. Internet traffic has become so congested that experts warn it could black out. Tape backup is essential to protect your website against loss.

Myths

"The Internet levels the playing field," is one axiom whose groove has worn so deep it's now a grave! It's the Internet's raw technology that allows everyone to use the same outlet for instantly reaching and selling anyone in the world, but that's where it stops. A playing field is far from level when small businesses are spending an average of $100,000 a year for Internet advertising and mid-size companies spend an average of $8,000,000. Still other rumors have websites costing an average of $1 million just to develop them!

Everyone wants to jump on the Internet money machine, and there isn't any reason why you can't too, providing you are not taken in by misleading sales presentations. The Internet does not offer a level playing field just like there isn't such as thing as a "free lunch." The key to success lies in your developing unique tactics for reaching, expanding and selling your market — strategies built into your eCommerce business plan.

Another misconception is that it doesn't cost very much money to start an eCompany. It isn't as expensive as opening a business on Main Street, but it does cost a considerable sum. For instance, Web designers and ISP's cost money. There are other expenses as well, securing a domain name, site maintenance, updating your software and hardware, spending a good portion of the workday keeping up with the Industry, selling your products, and answering emails. There is no such thing on the Web as "build it and they will come."

Myth number three is believing that listing your website with search engines ends your responsibility for driving traffic to your site. Search engines or portal sites maintain billions of pieces of data. Ending up as one of the lucky few within the first few Web pages takes know-how. So make certain your ISP or webmaster know how to move your business to the top Web page.

eTrends

Think about this! Man's entire knowledge warehouse can be contained in a space no larger than the head of a pin and then transmitted at white-hot speed. We have the know-how and it is rapidly becoming a reality. Forerunners to turning this achievement into practical everyday uses are already here saving businesses time and money. Three worth mentioning include wireless digital transmission, streaming media, and the Integrated On-Demand Network (ION) developed by Sprint.

If it seems unimportant to get your arms all the way around wireless delivery, perhaps cutting your telecommunication costs for a T-1 by 90 percent per month for speeds nearly four times faster will get your attention. According to Rami Hadar, CEO, Ensemble Communications *www.ensemblecom.com*, "We are at the beginning of a new era in wireless communications, a convergence of delivery systems. Business users can begin thinking in terms of one-stop-shopping for all their telecommunication needs. Instead of having a number of services such as a telephone company, an Internet service provider and different companies for voice mail, pagers and cell phones, users will have one provider and pay one bill. Consider this, a T-1 line today costs $400 a month on the low end and transmits 1.5MB per second. With wireless, the cost is reduced to $40 a month and has a Web transmission rate of 5MB per second.

Ensemble Communications is not alone, but is counted as a market leader among those who are developing the next generation, broadband wireless access. Its patented technology, Adaptix™, enables small and mid-size businesses to reduce costs for high-speed data/Internet access, video conferencing and all basic telephone services.

Streaming media is a catch-phrase for delivering content over the Internet that contains audio, video, graphics and text. The difference between an Internet media stream and television is interactivity, choice of content on the user's timetable not a broadcast station's, and the multitude of customized applications. Figuratively speaking, the Internet offers unlimited delivery "channels" versus the relative few channels available on broadcast television or the 100 or so channels on cable television.

The value streaming media brings to organizations and scholastic institutions globally is enormous. The opportunities streaming media offer to entrepreneurs is immense, something Larry St. John a seasoned broadcaster bet on in the early days of the Net. With more talent than investment capital, St. John zeroed in on a local technology market and has been distributing *San Diego Technology News*, *www.fresh-news.com*, over the Internet ever since. In October 1999, he took his business up the ladder several more rungs when he began streaming an audio and text version of the publication. According to St. John, other entrepreneurs wanting to tap into streaming media need to make certain their ISP has a Real Server or they need to buy their own. An ISP will charge between a $100 and $1,000 a month rent for stream capabilities.

Another innovative cost-cutting technology is ION. At speeds 100 times faster than today's conventional modems, ION allows users to make phone calls, send and receive faxes, and cruise the Internet at the same time over a single phone line. The added bonus is ION can reduce the cost of a typical telephone call by more than 70 percent. Moreover, it eliminates the need for multiple phone lines. Using ATM technology at speeds that load Web pages instantaneously, SprintION *www.sprint.com/ion* connects your company directly to the Internet backbone inexpensively. According to William T. Esrey, Sprint's chairman and CEO "A full-motion video call or conference between business associates will be less than to provide a typical domestic long distance phone call."

eTools

The following section describes different Internet applications to jump-start your software search for doing business electronically or to enable your asking the right questions of those who will be setting your eBusiness in motion. There are thousands of companies producing software equal to those listed and still thousands more offering industry-specific software. This is a light weight list at best and offered as a quick reference to begin the process of identifying what you need to launch your virtual empire.

DESCRIPTION	COMMENTS
Companies Are In Random Order	

ADVERTISING

GeoNet
www.adauction.com Zeros in on online media by targeting the customers that are relevant to your business.

AdKnowledge
www.focalink.com Focalink ad placement and reporting service specializing in the Web.

MatchLogic
www.matchlogic.com MatchLogic's proprietary targeting software manages ad campaigns for advertisers and their agencies by consolidating all campaign management functions.

DoubleClick
www.doubleclick.net DoubleClick/NetGravity is the equivalent of an advertising agency but operates exclusively on the Internet. The company targets markets and tests advertising for effectiveness — plus offers other related services.

L90.com
www.L90.com Company offers Internet advertising and direct marketing solutions such as consumer profiling, direct marketing packages, viral marketing initiatives, coupons, sweepstakes, customized sponsorships and content integration.

AUCTIONS

Bidland.com
www.bidland.com Bidland.com offers the enabling technology to get your company set up as an auction site in "less than an hour." Everything you need is automatically streamed to your company's site. This is another type of ASP (application service provider). See Internet Delivery.

DESCRIPTION	COMMENTS

CHAT ROOMS

Real Time Chat — *www.theforge.com* This program supports real-time chat room capabilities.

HearMe — *www.hearme.com* HearMe supports audio chat technology; a good idea for customer service departments or general use.

CUSTOMER SERVICE RESOURCE (CSR)

Internet Voice Technology — *www.net2phone.com* Incorporating voice technology into your website sales and customer service activities improves the efficiency and profitability of your site. net2Phone offers several products worth your time, e.g., real-time fax routing over the Internet, direct routing to your desktop or sales department.

CyberReps — *www.brigadesolutions.com* Brigade Solutions offer real people they call CyberReps to help your customers based on your requirements and knowledgebase.

eReps — *www.PeopleSupport.com* Called eReps, PeopleSupport answers your customers' questions via real-time chat, email or the phone.

Live Online Help — *www.facetime.net* FaceTime provides an interactive window that pops open on your customer's screen and lets a living person answer the customer's questions.

Voice and Video Calls — *www.visitalk.com* Visitalk.com adds a new twist to an in-house CSR and is compatible with other types of business communication over the Internet. They provide a free Permanent Communication Number (PCN) that becomes your individual Internet phone number. In addition, you are added to their Permanent Global Directory enabling you to find others and vice versa.

DEMOGRAPHIC AND OTHER RESEARCH

ZIP Code Demographics — *www.demographics.caci.com* CACI is an international tech firm offering ZIP code data services that includes population size, earnings, home costs and education levels.

Claritas Connect — *www.claritas.com* Claritas Connect is a reasonably priced yet sophisticated demographic search site.

Research-It — *www.iTools.com/research-it/research-it.html* Research-It is a quick one-stop reference tool.

DESCRIPTION	COMMENTS

DEMOGRAPHIC AND OTHER RESEARCH

Fedstats
www.fedstats.gov Maintains statistics from 70 U.S. federal government agencies including the Bureau of Labor Statistics. Search by demographic profile, region or government agency.

EDGAR
www.sec.gov/edgarhp.htm Electronic Data Gathering, Analysis and Retrieval System (EDGAR) a database of companies that file forms with the Securities and Exchange Commission with links to other sites.

Hoover's Online
www.hoovers.com A comprehensive website that mirrors the Hoover's directories for company profiles.

Reference
www.reference.com A reference source that lets you search the Usenet and mailing list archives, and newsgroup and mailing list directories. Order the results alphabetically or by preference. An excellent, well-organized resource.

DIGITAL WATERMARKING

Digimarc
www.digimarc.com Digimarc software imbeds an imperceptible watermark within an image that can reveal the author or distributor's complete contact details and copyright notice. It can also direct the user back to the author's website or point the user to websites as directed by the author or distributor.

EMAIL

Eudora
www.eudora.com Eudora Pro is a powerful email software offering many extras, such as, filtering, sending graphics images in the body of an email message.

InfoPress
www.castelle.com/ InfoPress Email-On-Demand software transforms your "info@" mailbox address into an automated, interactive e-mail system that allows users to request brochures, press releases or price lists via email and receive them within seconds automatically — a major cost savings. The software will also let you chose different document formats.

JetForm
www.jetform.com JetForm Workflow software, is a sophisticated tool that can email the work flow in a form format to the next person. Paper reduction and operating efficiency result.

DESCRIPTION   COMMENTS

EMAIL

Priority Email
www.fabrik.com Priority email is ideal for transmitting highly sensitive data. Fabrik Communications is one of the first companies to offer this service.

Real-Time Email Q&A
www.e-service.com We are all familiar with 800 customer service telephone calls. Now the same type of instant service is available on websites by installing E-Service software developed by Business Evolution. It lets customers type in questions while at your site and instantly receive a typed response from a real person .

FAX — FROM WEBSITE

Critical Path
www.cp.net Critical Path provides simple and secure Internet email, faxing, paging, and other messaging services for multiple users in a company. Reasonably priced, the service can substantially reduce overhead and consolidate telecommunication costs

VillageFax
www.sftek.com VillageFax offers business-to-business website-ready broadcast faxing.

INTERNET SERVICES

Application Service Provider
www.naviSite.com ASP's offer turnkey Web hosting and eCommerce solutions. You can buy as much or as little of any application that you need and only pay for what you use. The major advantage is not having capital tied up in software and hardware that becomes outdated shortly after it's installed. NaviSite is just one among hundreds of companies offering ASP services.

ASP for eBusiness
www.internetworking.gte.com GTE is a reliable Web hosting, extranet and intranet company offering a secure, scaleable infrastructure using Sun Technology.

Full Service ASP
www.xcelerate.com Offers the e-Business Supercenter™ with a single focus including interactive marketing, digital program management and Web design.

SmartAge
www.smartage.com An excellent ASP site for small businesses that don't want to go it alone.

DESCRIPTION	COMMENTS

LANGUAGE

LanguageWare   *www.languageware.net* The company is a "global eBusiness" that lets you create multilingual HTML Web pages.

LISTS AND NEWSGROUPS

ListBot   *www.listbot.com* ListBot is a free service that helps you generate return traffic, capture demographics and keep in touch with customers.

MANAGEMENT

SiteScape Forum   *www.sitescape.com* SiteScape Forum was specifically designed for team collaboration, distance learning, knowledge management and other corporate portal applications. Teams use it for reviewing their documents, obtaining approvals, sales lead workflow and similar Web-based collaboration.

PeopleSoft   *www.peoplesoft.com* PeopleSoft's Enterprise Performance Management software is designed to make your company operate more effectively by delivering relevant data for analysis, e.g., the over simplified grocery receipt example found on page 2. The obvious advantage is being able to make smarter decisions.

Productivity Software   *www.zkey.com* An all around tool that delivers an assortment of productivity applications such as Automated Form-Fill where users can enter their personal data once, an address book that self-updates by entering new numbers and updating old ones, a group calendar for sharing with team members plus obtaining real-time data on users, and more.

Document Management   *www.caere.com* Caere Corporation is one of the leading developers of software solutions for scanners and digital cameras. The company develops OCR, Web publishing, electronic forms, document management, and media asset management software.

Paperless Office   *www.paperless.com* The company offers an assortment of paper-to-digital conversion services for high-quality publications such as Internet and Intranet catalogs and brochures, presentations and custom databases, CD-ROM authoring, production and duplication.

DESCRIPTION	COMMENTS

MEDIA PLANNING

Telmar

www.telmar.com Telmar has a comprehensive media planning software for professional users.

MULTIMEDIA

Video Capture

www.b-way.com Broadway is an easy-to-install and use video capture, edit and a compression system that brings full-motion to flat/static presentations. It provides platform independence with plug-and-play capabilities. Video clip sample may be downloaded from the Web.

OPINION POLLING

Capture Opinions

www.o-pinion.com With just a click visitors may tell you what they like about your site and if it benefits them. Visit online opinion for a demonstration.

PUBLIC RELATIONS

Create Media Releases

www.digitalwork.lycos.com DigitalWork is a multi-duty service that helps with tasks like creating press releases or running credit checks.

SALES

WebWhacker

www.bluesquirrel.com The WebWhacker, developed by ForeFront Direct and maintained by BlueSquirrel, lets users whack their websites off the Net and store them on the hard drive.

WebCD

www.marketscape.com A multimedia WebCD motivates prospects and shortens sales cycles by allowing you to connect to the Net for live updates and transactions more effectively than your rivals.

brightware

www.brightware.com brightware offers a way to automate one-to-one marketing and sales dialogues in virtual companies by guiding eCustomers to purchase the best-suited products and services from your website.

DESCRIPTION	COMMENTS

SALES

UpShot.com
www.upshot.com UpShot is a hosted ASP sales service that provides sales team support from anywhere at anytime. This includes automatic forecasting, calendar sharing, contract management and industry news monitoring for a very reasonable monthly fee.

SEARCH ON WEBSITES

CommerceCourtLite *www.inex.com* This terrific software has a build-in search engine enabling your customers to find what they want when visiting your site. Another feature will automatically email you with a new order.

Free Navigational Service
www.freefind.com Is a large scale website search engine with a number of features including tracking visitors' searches, customization, and runs on FreeFind's servers so there is nothing for you to download or install. It can be added in 10 minutes to your website.

SECURITY

Internet Fraud
www.cybersource.com/fraud CyberSource is a well known specialist in Internet security issues. The CyberSource Internet Commerce Suite is a real-time back-office application that helps control credit card fraud to less than one percent.

Security Certification
www.icsa.net The Security Assurance Company takes the guess work out of website security by assuring both you and your customer of safety.

Secure Computing *www.securecomputing.com* Secure Computing has software applications that restrict or block incoming and outgoing messages as well as selected website access. This type of software is particularly important if companies want to curtail Internet abuse among employees or make certain areas are off limits altogether, such as, bookkeeping and personnel. Software alone is not fail-proof, though. Security software ranges in price from around $50 to over $8,000.

SHOPPING CARTS

JustAddCommerce *www.richmediatech.com* This software does double duty by supporting multiple currencies as well as letting you add a shopping cart system to your site.

DESCRIPTION   **COMMENTS**

SHOPPING CARTS

Shopping Cart Professional

www.webgenie.com Lets customers access the current status of their orders as well as supports different foreign languages.

Miva

www.miva.com Miva provides eCommerce solutions for a variety of needs, e.g., shopping carts, etc.

STREAMING MEDIA

Akamai

www.akamai.com Akamai Technologies, Inc. is a new and unique service provider that is transforming website delivery for streaming media. Developed by MIT computer scientists, the breakthrough algorithms intelligently rout and replicate content over large network servers versus centralized servers. It lets us use tomorrow's technology today by supporting the most "heavily trafficked and content-rich websites in the world."

TELEPHONE

Internet

www.vocaltec.com The Internet Phone, from VocalTec, allows company members or outsiders with an Internet Phone to easily chat with each other over the Web.

UPDATING SOFTWARE

Software Update Finder

www.mcafee.com Formally called Oil Change, the Software Update Finder tracts new releases or upgrades for applications already installed on your computer. It will also automatically download and install the updated version.

WAREHOUSING

NCR

www.ncr.com

EMC

www.emc.com These two companies offer large capacity data warehousing services suited to most any requirement.

WEBSITE DEVELOPMENT

WebBurst

www.powerproduction.com WebBurst is among other state-of-the-art developed by PowerProduction Software. This cutting-edge multimedia

DESCRIPTION	COMMENTS

WEBSITE DEVELOPMENT

authoring software tool is "simple enough for non-technical beginners yet powerful enough for the pro's" for creating dynamic Webpages using JAVA.

Java Commerce Tool Kit

www.sun.com A professional tool that simplifies website development

Fusion

www.netobjects.com Fusion, a website development software, is easier than others to use and can adapt to an assortment of development tools.

ecBuilderPro

www.ecbuilder.com ecBuilder Pro software is designed to help you create your company's website and then automatically submit it to major Internet search engines.

OTHER

Modems

www.zyxel.com ZyXEL makes excellent modems and is a leading supplier of high speed professional equipment that connects users to the Internet. For instance, a company might have ten users in an office. Each is connecting to the Internet from different locations. Their telephone lines need to be routed into a central location. ZyXEL is known for their "routing" equipment and other related products.

The Office Pod

www.haworth-furn.com An office pod is a collapsible piece of furniture requiring minimum storage space. When opened, it offers a fully functional work area. One of the best examples was developed by Haworth Furniture Company and is priced between $1,500 and $2,000. The pod will pay for itself in less than a year when weighing the investment against the cost of office space.

Email Only Appliance

If email only is all you need on the road or anytime for that matter, there are several appliances on the market ranging in price from just under $100 to about $400, but do come with a few compromises. The Sharp TM-20/PocketMail weighs only eight ounces and is available from pocketmail.com. InfoGear's iPhone offers phone, answering machine, email and Web browser and looks like a well designed desk phone. The iPhone is available from major retail electronic stores. The CIDCO MailStation comes ready to plug into a phone jack with all of your user ID and is available from CIDCO Internet Service.

How to Use This Book
to Write Your Plan

What to Expect from this Book

eCommerce notwithstanding, preparing a business plan takes time, thought and effort. Yours should be an original not a cookie cutter of some other plan. In fact, it is hopeless to even attempt to raise funds from plans that are obviously copied, too wordy, boilerplate, sloppy, or poorly thought out.

Although the five-year business plan is standard, three-year plans are also popular. Based upon older paradigms, five-year planning cycles used proven business models, and therefore, were more predictable. Today, however, flexibility is key if you want to stay competitive in our lightning-fast, technology-driven marketplace. Develop your planning cycle accordingly.

There are three types of business plans. The first primarily seeks venture capital (VC), the second a business loan, and the third serves as part of a broader plan known as a prospectus. The primary difference among all three is the financial wording, with the exception of the legal text found in a prospectus. A VC-seeking plan addresses issues describing the investors' company involvement and financial benefits, while a debt-seeking plan focuses on the banker's five-Cs of credit: character, credit, cash flow, capacity and collateral. A prospectus is needed to sell stock in a company. Plans can also be a combination of all three.

It is somewhat of a toss-up as to who has the toughest requirements for funding a business — an investor or a banker. Each is different. Investors will take far more risks than a bank, sometimes buying into the company based on the value of an idea. Banks, on the other hand, require collateral before lending money. In either case, you can't even get the process started without a business plan.

Creating a practical and successful plan, though, is just the beginning, since it also acts as a blueprint for managing the company. It isn't meant to sit on a shelf after the company has been funded. You must work the plan, so make sure it is workable.

To make your plan workable for your business, don't gloss over your company's strengths and weaknesses. Find ways to expand on its strengths while overcoming its weaknesses. Expanding on a strength might mean making a good product great.

Overcoming a weakness might mean developing a strategic alliance with a company whose strengths compensate for your weaknesses. Also, don't over plan. In a volatile and ever expanding global marketplace, give yourself room to miss the mark or change your mind by designating alternate courses of action when needed.

Although nearly everyone familiar with business plans agrees on what needs to be in a plan, there isn't a hard and fast rule for the order in which information is presented. The order shown in this book was chosen with an eye toward including all vital information versus providing a sequential formula; it is, however, a recognized format and may be followed with confidence. If this format does not quite fit your business, though, rearrange it so it does.

There are eight sections to the business plan in this book. As shown in Example 2, each section represents one plan chapter and begins with a chapter title, followed by a list of chapter contents. This is followed by a brief explanation of the section's objectives and then the Business Plan Sequence, which is laid out on a scheme sheet. Figuratively speaking, scheme sheets provide a visual table of contents.

EXAMPLE 2

Writing the Business Plan

SECTION ONE

I. INTRODUCTION
1. Business Description
2. Executive Summary

Section One Objectives

This section provides your reader with a highlighted description of your business and captures the main points of the plan in an Executive Summary. Beginning with the cover page and working forward through, and including, section one, the plan is laid out in the following sequence.

Business Plan Sequence

Cover Page	Inside Cover Page	Optional Preface	Table of Contents	Blank Sheet	Title INTRODUCTION I. Business Description	2. Executive Summary

---

If you are not familiar with scheme sheets, the idea for using this format was borrowed from the print media. Publications use a sheet of paper that has a number of blank rectangles on it. Each rectangle represents one page. Key words are used to note the content for that page. It is easier to view a format and its contents for a large document on a few pages than to keep flipping through the manuscript.

The Business Plan Sequence illustrated on the scheme sheet is followed by a short introductory paragraph. A bulleted short list of instructions entitled "Writer's

Checklist" follows the chapter subheading. It was written for you, the business plan writer, as a quick reference to see if all of the information you selected is included.

One paragraph of sample text for each chapter subheading follows the writer's checklist as shown in Example 3. This format is consistent throughout enabling anyone to produce a polished document without the typical frustration.

EXAMPLE 3

I. INTRODUCTION
1. Business Description

Writer's Checklist

- Present three or four compact sentences in the first paragraph.
- Only include pertinent details.
- In the second paragraph, state your company's funding objectives.
- If needed, add a third paragraph with applicable investor information.
- Keep the Business Description to one page or less — preferably, one half to three quarters of a page.

SAMPLE TEXT

Existing Company

NyTec Corporation manufactures fasteners for software packaging. The company was established in 1989 with the introduction of its Easy Close brand, incorporated in 1992, and has grown from $xx in gross annual sales the first year to $xxx million the last fiscal. Over the last eighteen months, NyTec has successfully developed, patented, and tested two new snap-lock fasteners for software packaging, identified three new marketing opporunities, reshaped its organizational structure, and created a Website in preparation of its planned expansion. Projections show this will increase NyTec's profit margin by xx percent while improving efficiencies, customer service, deliveries, and accelerate growth by another xx percent.

A fictitious company named NyTec plays the starring role here. Following NyTec's planning strategy in the sample text, helps to clarify ways that you might choose to integrate eCommerce activities into your overall strategy. In many instances, the sample text can be customized to fit your business, but of itself, is not meant to be all-inclusive. It is meant to show how text is written in a plan and illustrate how the Internet is used in a company. More often than not, you will need to write your own text and several additional paragraphs to present your ideas.

Blank worksheets are provided in the back of the book for this purpose. Their titles and numbers correspond to subheadings in the business plan. Many of the worksheet examples in the text have been completed and are provided as guides to give you an idea as to how you can develop and organize information prior to writing the plan. Worksheets that are self-explanatory are not included in the text as examples.

A typical table of contents for a business plan is provided in Appendix A. It is handy to make several copies so you can scratch through, add to, and rearrange chapter titles and subheadings. You are also encouraged to write down every detail using the blank worksheets. When you're finished flushing out ideas, making notes, and writing draft copy, these worksheets can easily be removed from this book and used as a comprehensive resource for completing the final business plan.

Some plan sections provide a chapter summary with sample text. Summaries, though optional, are helpful for highlighting how the information ties together in logical sequence. Summaries are also ideal short-cut presentations for advisory board members, designated personnel, and others when complete business plans are, quite frankly, too expensive or confidential to distribute. When linked together with the plan's Introduction, chapter summaries obviously offer more detail than just an Executive Summary. Selected charts and graphs can be included forming a quick, yet comprehensive, presentation — a mini-plan, so to speak.

If used as a mini-plan, assemble the presentation with a cover page that differs from that of the complete business plan. Include names, addresses, and contact numbers on the second page, followed by a table of contents. Follow with an optional blank sheet, the Introduction and then chapter summaries. Eliminate the Executive Summary. Keep chapter summaries to one-half page or less. Excluding the cover and first two or three sheets, the presentation should be less than ten pages. And believe it or not, your mini-plan can be further condensed to just one page.

One-page summaries are invaluable for disseminating to business associates who will benefit from your vision, for educating certain personnel, and for querying investors or bankers. If used for a funding query, the one-page brief acts somewhat like an ad, allowing potential investors to quickly decide if they are interested in your venture or not. It saves an enormous amount of time. An example is provided in Appendix B.

If you have read other business plan writing books, to avoid confusion it is worth mentioning that some professional plan developers title the opening section "Background" or "Summary" versus "Introduction." Other headings and subheadings may vary from plan to plan as well. It is a matter of professional style. Don't become too engrossed in semantics since plan titles are moot in the first place. The idea is to develop a strong case for your business that is easily understood. Words alone will not attract investors, motivate employees or secure business loans. Facts will. So deliver rational, fact-filled, goal-driven information in a clear writing style.

This will attract investors or rally an enthusiastic team of managers, employees, and associates behind you. One note of caution avoid industry jargon, verbosity, big words, and flowery writing styles.

As for trade secrets, you do not have to supply them in your plan or discuss them with anyone. However, most investors and sometimes bankers will insist on knowing in order to evaluate the merits of the venture. Use caution, common sense, and legal counsel, if needed, prior to exposing highly competitive trade secrets. Also, check with your attorney, you might be able to patent your business method.

Other tools in this book that will come in handy include a glossary of business and Internet terms. On the light side, when writers block strikes, and it will, turn to the last page of the glossary. There you will find comic relief in the "Jargon Generator," anonymously created by a Sweetwater, Texas high school district administrator who, no doubt, finds humor in business-term verbosity.

Success Lessons You Already Know

Unfortunately, success doesn't come with either a formula or a guarantee. If it did, every idea would become a success story by way of a business plan and every plan would be funded immediately by way of a guaranteed checklist. Navigating the road to success also requires know-how, intuition, patience, wisdom, and common sense — the kind you get from driving any metropolitan freeway. In fact, applying this navigational experience to steering your business upward exposes ten practical success-lessons you already know.

Lesson One: Don't Cut In!

On and off ramps to freeways are often heavily congested during rush hours. Long lines of cars snail along. Just as you reach the off ramp, a driver cuts in front of you from the fast lane. Not only can this cause an accident; the driver hasn't earned the right to be there.

Business is like that. Jumping ahead of yourself increases the chance of failure. Companies go under from growing too fast just as easily as they do from not growing at all. It simply takes time to earn your place in line. Success is built on integrity in the marketplace, a good company image, finding and keeping responsible employees, developing dependable supplier-partnering resources, and loyal customers. You can't buy these goodwill assets. They must be earned and that takes time. "Mean what you say, say what you mean, and do what you say."

Lesson Two: Stay Awake.

Falling asleep at the wheel invites calamity. Highly effective business leaders are alert to what is going on around them. They watch the bottom line and shifts in the marketplace; if either shows signs of waning, they take action. Not only are leaders awake, they encourage everyone around them to stay awake by promoting value for value, fair play and healthy attitudes among everyone in the organization. Create a reliable feedback loop, one that provides sufficient information for making sound decisions.

Lesson Three: Don't be a Road Hog.
Be Willing to Give Others the Right of Way.

You need to exit the freeway. With turn signals blinking you try to change lanes, but no one is willing to slow down, even a little, and let you in. This is a lot like poor customer service. When companies wear blinders and are too busy to be bothered, customers get the message and take their business elsewhere. Customer loyalty isn't won because a company has the best ad campaign, product, or service. Customers are loyal because companies understand the importance of letting them have the right of way.

Lesson Four: Don't Drive With Your Eyes Glued on the Rear View Mirror.

Obviously, this invites disaster. Last year's model might not work this year. Yesterday's way of operating a company may be outdated. In truth, yesterday doesn't exist. Its only claim on today is how we remember the experience. Head-in-the-sand management has knocked many giant corporations out of the ball game; countries too — remember Rome! Use your rear view mirror for glancing, but only long enough to use what you gained from experience as a way to successfully go forward.

Lesson Five: Obey the Rules. Stop Means Stop.

There are certain unwritten rules of business that have grown up over time. Companies that ignore these rules sometimes find themselves in a great deal of trouble. One of these rules is that entering the marketplace too soon can be as big a financial bath as entering it too late. When markets are too new, customers must be educated about a product's value. This is costly with no guarantee of customer acceptance. Entering a market too late is equally costly. It takes a lot of money to be heard over the roar of a crowd even when a product or service is vastly superior. Timing is important to business success.

Lesson Six: Don't Sweat the Traffic Jams, Roadblocks, and Detours.

Not only are all industries cyclic, unforeseen events occur causing traffic jams, roadblocks, and detours. When you allow yourself to get upset at these times, you simply deplete your power to take control and find a way around the problem. If you have to pace the floor, decide you will for 15 minutes. After that, decide you are going to roll up your sleeves, look the problem square in the face, and tackle it right then and there. If you just sit there fuming, you're going to grow an even bigger problem.

Lesson Seven: Invest in Good Tires.

Ridding on shabby tires is risky. So is being under capitalized. It frays your nerves and causes you to make snap judgments to solve money problems. Not only should you have enough working capital, but it is equally important to find financial partners, bankers included, who share your same vision and are willing to help you safely arrive at your destination.

Lesson Eight: Keep Your Car in Good Condition.

Clunkers aren't dependable and certainly won't get you very far. Poorly planned strategies are like clunkers. You can't depend on them to get you where you want to go. You need solid, no-nonsense, realistic plans that stack the odds of succeeding in your favor. You also need to keep your equipment up to speed. Old equipment, like clunkers, will hold your company back far quicker than any competitor can. Out-of-date equipment and software are costly. They are slower and can break down any time, causing unplanned downtime.

Lesson Nine: Be a Responsible Driver.

If you take the responsibility of sitting behind the wheel, you not only have to look where you're going, but watch out for other drivers as well. Support and encourage everyone in your organization — particularly your sales team. Make it easy for sales people to contact prospects, negotiate, and sell your products or services. Provide the direction and share company objectives, then coach, coach, coach. Motivate your team so they will want to play the game to win.

Watching out for others also means becoming community minded. Whether your company is part of a neighborhood or the international business community, it needs to think about helping to improve the very community that buys its products or services. All nonprofit organizations need donor support either in time, money, or both. Involvement not only has its own reward, it keeps a business's name before customers, promotes goodwill, enhances a company's image, and internalizes a charitable philosophy. Some companies even start their own nonprofit organization to support worthy causes. Overall, businesses with a charitable mindset make a statement advertising cannot buy.

Lesson Ten: Keep Up With the Flow of Traffic.

To be safe on a freeway, you need to drive at the speed of traffic — to keep up with the flow. Drivers in slow lanes with white knuckles aren't any safer. Don't let fear hold you back. Sometimes, it's necessary to cut loose, to go for it even if you have to briefly exceed the speed limit. These are judgment calls. Successful leaders know when to drive slow or speed up. They are driven by know-how, talent, experience, and vision — not fear.

And when you finally pull off the freeway and into a multistory parking building, take a top-story mindset with you because there is "always room at the top. It's the bottom that's crowded." Businesses, like drivers, are pretty easy to read if you know what to look for. Any busy weekend you'll find a parking structure full of business lessons.

There are drivers on the first floor who are willing to wait for a shopper to exit the mall, make her way to her car and finally relinquish that coveted parking space. Some of these drivers-in-waiting block oncoming traffic and others pull over letting cars pass. It really doesn't make any difference; the point is that these drivers are not interested in moving up. They have a first-floor-mindset. There's nothing wrong with this; it's just that the first floor is very crowed, has less opportunity, and makes business success more difficult.

Other drivers have driven on to the second or third floors. More aggressive, these drivers are adamant about getting a space where someone is pulling out — supposedly. The driver pulling out usually takes his or her time and the flow of traffic is held up. Some businesses are like this, unlike the drivers-in-waiting who gamble that sales will come their way if they wait long enough, these companies are aggressive, but are still willing to wait — just in a different way and with fewer limits and crowds.

If, on the other hand, you're a driver who has a top-floor mindset, you patiently follow your plan with conviction, arrive on the top floor, and 95 percent of the time, pull into a space next to the entry. You had a plan, followed through, and didn't limit yourself because you knew there were plenty of parking spaces on top.

General Guidelines for a Finished Plan

Finally, don't underplay the finished product. It speaks volumes about you and the company in general. Your finished business plan should:

- Demonstrate overall professionalism.
- Be neatly prepared, assembled, and bound.
- Be edited (professionally if possible) for clarity, organization, grammar and spelling.
- Have a cover page with a proprietary caution that the plan is not to be reproduced, and if on loan, to be returned. Provide a stamped, self-addressed large envelope for this purpose
- Identify your company by name, address, email address, fax, telephone, contact person, and if applicable, your URL.
- Have a number, such as 1 of 10.
- Have a Table of Contents with figures, charts, tables, and exhibits listed.
- Be 40 pages or less including the Appendices.

- Have an Executive Summary that covers all major aspects.
- Have all figures, exhibits, and tables referenced in the plan's text.
- Substantiate everything you claim with footnotes; the footnote should identify the information source with a date, and if applicable, page number(s) where the resource can be found.
- Clearly exhibit all appropriate legal disclaimers as they apply to the plan and financial forecasts.

Input from outside professionals, such as an attorney, accountant, banker, insurance advisor, technocrat, or other specialists may also prove helpful. The end result will produce an individualized and successful eCommerce business plan positioned to stay the course.

Writing the Business Plan

SECTION ONE

I. INTRODUCTION
1. Business Description
2. Executive Summary

Section One Objectives

This section provides your reader with a highlighted description of your business and captures the main points of the plan in an Executive Summary. Beginning with the cover page and working forward through, and including, section one, the plan is laid out in the following sequence.

Business Plan Sequence

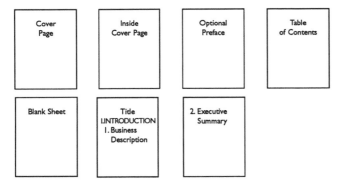

As previously mentioned in the instructions the preceding format introduces each of the plan's eight sections. Taking a few minutes to review all eight sections, will help you quickly grasp how a business plan is structured for most business types. Although nearly everyone familiar with business plans agrees on what needs to be in a plan, there isn't a hard and fast rule for the order in which information is presented. The order shown in this book was chosen with an eye toward including all vital information versus providing an iron-clad sequential formula; it is, however, a recognized format and may be followed with confidence. If any of the sections discussed in businessplan.com do not fit your business, rearrange the format to suit your company. An explanation of the Business Plan Sequence follows:

Cover Page: As with any bound report, the title or cover page identifies your company and the title of the document, for example, NyTec Corporation and underneath, Five-Year Business Plan. You may also want to add the preparer's name(s), your legal and accounting affiliations, or other related associates. In the lower right hand corner write the following: "This Plan is 1 of 10," indicating the number of plans in print. Underneath, write the word "Confidential." If expense is not a concern, you may want to use a custom cover.

Inside Cover Page: Repeat the information on the inside cover page adding your contact numbers and those for your associates shown on the cover page. Include the date. If the plans are assigned, write, in the lower right hand corner, "This confidential plan is assigned to C. J. Turner."

Optional Preface: The inside cover page is followed by an optional preface. The preface might contain information that does not fit, or cannot be found elsewhere in the plan. Be brief, keeping the text to one page or less.

Table of Contents: As you are developing the plan, keep a list of its contents; for apparent reasons, though, the table of contents is written last. Some word processing software programs let users automatically track contents making it easier to develop a Table of Contents as the text is written or changes are made.

Blank Sheet: An optional blank page may be added to separate the preceding pages from the body of the plan.

First Page: Title the plan by stating the name of your company and whether the plan is for three or five years. Center the title at the top of the first page as shown Figure 1.1. Adding your logo is graphically pleasing providing the size is balanced with the overall appearance.

FIGURE 1.1

NyTec CORPORATION
Five-Year Business Plan
2001 to 2005

The first section of a plan begins with the introduction, followed by a brief description of the business and then, an Executive Summary. Think of these pages as your commercial that captures the most pertinent information about the company in two to three pages. Ironically, information for the first section is compiled as the plan is developed and written last. The reason, of course, is obvious. Bottom line objectives emerge after the planning process, not before.

Roman numerals were chosen for chapter headings. Numbers and upper and lower case are used for subheadings as shown. Like the plan's sequential order, this numbering combination is a matter of personal preference. Any numbering format may be used providing it is consistent and will not confuse readers.

After the title, begin by writing, I. INTRODUCTION, and then, 1. Business Description, followed by the text. A writer's checklist is provided as a quick reference and further explained in detail following the sample text.

I. INTRODUCTION
1. Business Description

Writer's Checklist

- Keep the Business Description to one page or less — preferably, one-half to three-quarters of a page.
- Present three or four compact sentences in the first paragraph.
- Only include pertinent details.
- In the second paragraph, state your company's funding objectives.
- If needed, add a third paragraph with applicable investor information.

SAMPLE TEXT

Existing Company

NyTec Corporation manufactures fasteners for software packaging. The company was established in 1989 with the introduction of its Easy Close brand, incorporated in 1992, and has grown from $xx in gross annual sales the first year to $xxx million the last fiscal. Over the last 18 months, NyTec has successfully developed, patented, and tested two new snap-lock fasteners for software packaging, identified three new marketing opportunities, reshaped its organizational structure, and created a website in preparation of its planned expansion. Projections show this will increase NyTec's profit margin by xx percent while improving efficiencies, customer service, deliveries, and accelerate growth by another xx percent.

SAMPLE TEXT

Proposed Company

NyTec, is a proposed corporation that will manufacture software packaging that uses a patented snap-lock fastener developed by the National Aeronautic and Space Alliance (NASA). Three founders have invested $xx and 18 months obtaining an exclusive license from NASA, developing pre-marketing opportunities, and acquiring a major account valued at $xxx over a 12-month period. Based on these activities, the company projects gross sales in its second year of $xxx million and an average annual growth rate of 20 percent thereafter.

The first paragraph of your business plan should capture a reader's attention and contain no more than four carefully constructed sentences. Notice how the sentences in the sample text are written. The first highlights the company's background by going right to the point. The following sentence lets readers know what the company has accomplished and what it intends to do. The last two sentences describe how these accomplishments will improve the company. These opening statements provide all of the necessary framework you need. They act as anchor points for providing more details throughout the plan.

If the plan is also being developed as a funding proposal, the second and third paragraphs describe company objectives, pertinent financial data, and state the amount of funds requested. If yours is a venture capital seeking plan, state the anticipated return on investment (ROI) and major points of the exit strategy, if any. An exit strategy suggests how you and the investors will part company, if at all. For a full-text Exit Strategy example, please refer to Section VIII: Financial Plan.

The following text examples illustrate how financial narratives can be kept to a minimum and still be effective. However, you are cautioned to seek legal counsel for matters concerning all forms of funding, and specifically, how this information is written in a plan. Protecting your company from lawsuits at the onset is less expensive than leaving the door open to costly litigation later. Worksheet 1: Business Description in the back of the book, is provided for noting ideas about your company and writing a business description. Use the sample text as a guide.

SAMPLE TEXT

Exit Strategy

In the event that any or all investors choose to discontinue their financial interest in the company at the end of the xx-month period, NyTec offers to repurchase the investors' shares at a total price equal to xx percent (or the percentage ownership represented by the shares tendered) of the value of the company as indicated by the

Common Stock and Retained Earnings levels in the balance sheet. Based on current financial projections, this stock repurchase will substantially increase the return realized by investors.

SAMPLE TEXT

Investment Proposal

This business plan is to demonstrate to investors the financial merits of investing in NyTec, thereby, participating in the returns generated from its patented products. The new capital commitment of $xx million will be dispersed over the first 6 months. It will be used to further develop additional technical products, increase personnel and expand the company's marketing activities described herein. In return, investors will receive xx percent interest in the company and one board seat. Based on current financial projections and a xx percent share in distributed earnings, investors will receive an attractive xxx percent return on their initial investment over the proposed 36-month period. This significant return will be further enhanced by the investors' share ownership in the increasing value of the company.

SAMPLE TEXT

Risk Considerations

NyTec is a new company without any track record. It has completed all start-up activities and is awaiting additional funding to implement its business described in this plan. The investor should also consider that this plan is based on future events that may or may not occur regardless of best efforts put forth. There is no guarantee that any sales projections will incorporate actual events. Investors should carefully consider these risks and consult with their own legal and financial advisors.

---

2. Executive Summary

Writer's Checklist

- Narrative text or bulleted points are acceptable.
- Keep text to a maximum of three pages; two pages are better.
- Avoid industry jargon.
- Clearly define your company's major selling points, such as:
  - your marketing plan,

    - management team's qualifications,

    - and highlighted financial data.

SAMPLE TEXT

Executive Summary

The following highlighted information is explained in detail throughout NyTec's business plan. (Follow with a bulleted list or narrative text.)

The primary objective of the Executive Summary is to enable investors, bankers, and managers to quickly grasp the essence of the business plan without having to wade through the whole document. If more details on a particular topic are needed, a reader can easily refer to that section of the plan.

Major points become obvious as research is completed and strategies identified. It is easier if you compile these main points as you go along; editing and formatting can be done later. When you're developing this list, make a pencil note in the margin where the information is located in the plan. It saves time later on when pulling your business plan together.

Some plans present Executive Summaries in a narrative style while others choose a bulleted list. Either way is acceptable, but keep the summary to a few pages, bringing the entire first section to less than three or four pages. Remember, this is your commercial. The reader needs to understand the concept and be sold in the first few pages. For this reason, you are also encouraged to polish Section One to a fault. In fact, tackle it with the same gusto a copy writer would an ad campaign. The end result won't look like an ad, of course, but that is exactly what it is — a sales tool you can use to excite others about your company. Use Worksheet 2: Executive Summary in the back of the book to collect the main points as you develop the plan.

Worksheet 3: Business Information, will be helpful in the formation stages of developing your plan. Don't be too concerned if the information seems somewhat irrelevant or a little foreign at the moment. It will all come together, step-by-step, as you will soon see. A corresponding blank worksheet is provided in the back of the book.

WORKSHEET 3: Business Information

My Enterprise: .com _X_ .edu ___ . gov ___ .org. ___ other _____

Number of Employees: _____27 with 18 on site and 9 who telecommute_____

_____

Number of Locations: ___10___ Where: Headquarters, 6 U.S. regional sales _____ sites, 2 in Canada, 1 in London (Remind myself to get addresses from _____ William)_____

Website: Yes _X_ No _____ Planning to have _____

_____

Internet Service Provider: _____ Name: ACD NetConnect _____

Address: _____ 1234 North Maple Avenue, Township, Idaho 12345 _____

_____

Phone: _____ (111) 123-4567 Fax: (111) 123-4568 _____

Email: _____ acd@netconnect.com _____

My URL: ___ www.nytec.com _____

Need Email _____ All personnel. _____

Filter/Security Software: Yes _X_ No _____ $1,500 price range +/−

What's Blocked: _ Personnel records; company financials; banking; research _____ and development work; trade secrets; sensitive marketing data. The ISP _____ mentioned we might need to upgrade our firewall. I need to talk this over _____ with Max. _____

Who's Blocked: _____ All personnel will be blocked from accessing the above _____ except those directly involved in the work. Note: I want the website to be _____ open to the public and also be private as described above. _____

_____

SECTION TWO

II. PRODUCTS AND SERVICES
1. Description and Benefits
2. Product Mix by Ratio to Sales

Section Two Objectives

Section Two is show and *sell*. It provides the reader with a detailed description of your products, the services you offer, and how much each product group generates in revenue. Section Two is laid out in the following sequence.

Business Plan Sequence

Assume for a moment that your business plan is completed and being read by a potential investor. The first two or three pages sparked his or her imagination, creating a genuine interest in your company. Each section, from this point forward, needs to bolster that initial interest while reinforcing the plan's credibility. Begin Section Two by presenting both a narrative and graphic (if applicable) description of your products and services. Also, explain why your products benefit, or will benefit, your customers. A writer's checklist is provided as a quick reference, and is further explained in detail following the sample text. References to Figures or Appendices in sample text models are fictitious.

II. PRODUCTS AND SERVICES
1. Description and Benefits

Writer's Checklist

- Describe your products and services along with customer benefits in two or three paragraphs.
- Briefly outline your eCommerce advantage (further described in the sample text).
- Note any patents, trademarks or copyrights held by your company. Copies of these may be exhibited in the Appendices (optional).
- Provide product illustrations or photocopies when appropriate, and/or refer the reader to them in the Appendices.

SAMPLE TEXT

Description and Benefits

NyTec's established Easy Close fastener line features two models, an envelope slip closure and a slip and snap closure. The two new patented fasteners were designed for direct mail and single disk storage software packaging. This new brand, the Sure Lock, has far-reaching applications since the fasteners are integrated into custom designed packaging for customers. In addition to pilferage-free packaging, customers benefit from the company's in-house graphic design group who are recognized for their award-winning designs and rapid turnaround.

NyTec's website additionally enhances its marketing position. Customers are given unique pin codes that allow private access to a website created especially for viewing their packaging in 3-D graphics. Customers can manipulate their packaging, change colors and sizes, and make comments that are emailed back to the design team at NyTec. When a design meets with the customer's approval, he or she can make a selection and place an order. If a deposit is required, customers are offered several payment methods, including secure credit card transactions.

Detailed throughout this plan, operating costs have been reduced by up to xx percent for reaching and servicing customers, distributing product literature, project sharing among employees and other internal activities, such as those related to human resources. The patented snap and lock feature also cuts assembly labor costs by as much as xx percent. The end result is a quality product at a cost xx percent less than the nearest competitor. Product photocopies are shown on the following page, Figure xx, featuring the Easy Close and the Sure Lock. Patent information is available to qualified investors.

NyTec has successfully described its products and stated its customer benefits. The reader now knows the company has an award-winning design team, an unique interactive involvement with packaging design and a convenient ordering system that customers may opt to use. The reader has also been told that the company has an established fastener brand and two new patented fasteners ready for market. Additionally, the fasteners are less expensive than similar products.

It is easy to see why most customers will want to do business with NyTec. It is also easy to see why some companies get funded and others don't. In this instance, investors and bankers will immediately see the company's value.

But before you reach out and grab the reader's imagination with colorful product graphics and magazine-worthy text, there are a few simple rules to keep in mind. Experience has shown that companies have a tendency to overkill this part of the plan, in part, because it is easy to become enamored with their products — akin to parents who wear rose-colored glasses. On the surface, explaining every detail seems rational, and a good way to transfer the same excitement to an audience. The danger is that too much information usually yields confusion and the opposite reaction from readers. Consequently, readers often draw wrong conclusions. You don't want this to happen, particularly with an investor or banker.

Note too, how the preceding sample text is factual, provable and, therefore, believable. It allows readers to draw their own conclusions while creating a successful company image. Neither NyTec nor its audience can be misled. Try to be impartial as you begin writing your business plan. If you have a tendency to wear rose colored glasses, take them off and view your products from your customer's viewpoint. If readers are led to draw favorable conclusions as they delve deeper into your plan, they will be motivated by their own enthusiasm to "jump on your band wagon."

Withhold altogether and/or put supporting documents, such as patents, trademarks, copyrights, or elaborate drawings, etc., in the Appendices. If applicable, provide a half- or-full-page exhibit of your products in a figure and cross reference it in the text. Other do's and don'ts include the following:

Do

- Use high quality photocopies of photographs or drawings of the products.
- Identify each product (group or brand) by name.
- For large product lines only select a few best sellers for display in the plan. Reference the other products and offer your product catalog on request.

Do not

- Use product photographs pasted on a sheet of paper as a way to illustrate the line.
- Use photographs enclosed in clear plastic cover sheets.
- Use sales brochures or catalog sheets in place of text and product illustrations.
- Use cluttered amateur-type illustrations.
- Provide more than one page of product graphics in the body of the plan.

This section of the business plan should not look like a sales catalog, which can always be provided under separate cover. When in doubt, lean toward a conservative format. A service firm wanting to include graphics, might opt to explain its product by using small icons for each type of service. The same approach may be used for a tangible product line as well. Original icons developed by a commercial artist are recommended, though, versus clip art. Your plan's content should lead a reader forward quickly, not break his or her concentration with lengthy details and hard to understand graphics or schematics.

The preceding sample text also references different ways a company can utilize the Internet: one, as a cost-savings tool and the other, for customer conveniences and services. If you have a website, most likely you will find it easy to write a description of its cost-saving value and customer benefits unique to your company. Rely on a few notes from Section One, to help out here and should you need to, revisit Worksheet 3: Business Information.

If your website is still in the creation phase, you might want to skip the Internet-related text for the moment, and come back to it later. Worksheet 4: Description and Benefits, is provided in the back of the book. Jot down ideas as they come to you. These ideas can be used later when you are writing the copy for this section.

2. Product Mix by Ratio to Sales

Writer's Checklist

- Categorize your products or, if a service firm, your services.
- Provide the past three years sales activities by product mix.
- If describing a proposed company, identify the product mix and estimate what each category will contribute to overall sales projections.
- An optional graph or chart may be used to illustrate the product mix by ratio to sales.

SAMPLE TEXT

Product Mix by Ratio to Sales

NyTec offers four different packaging closures in 15 sizes and four colors. Figure x, shows the company's product mix by ratio to sales for the past three years for its standard Easy Close brand with five-year sales projections for the new patented Sure Lock brand. As the new line gains in popularity, the company anticipates a sales decline for its older Easy Close line.

The idea behind grouping products together is straight forward, it's easier to track sales for a group of products than individual units. If you haven't already, identify

WORKSHEET 5: Product Mix By Ratio to Sales

Product Mix	Percent of Sales Past Performance			Projected				
	1998	1999	2000	2001	2002	2003	2004	2005
<u>Sure Lock</u>								
Single Disk Storage	N/A	N/A	N/A	17%	22%	27%	32%	35%
Mailers	N/A	N/A	N/A	14%	18%	21%	25%	31%
<u>Easy Close</u>								
Envelope Slip	56%	52%	44%	31%	22%	17%	12%	7%
Slip & Snap	44%	48%	56%	38%	38%	35%	31%	27%

all similar products and create a category for each group. Provide sales percentages for at least the past three years together with your projections. If your company does not have a track record, estimate what each group will contribute as a percentage of projected gross sales.

Although not necessary for inclusion in a plan, types of products, and brands within product types may be measured against each other and tied into your financial software and database. Most accountants or your information systems manager can set this up for you. These records will let you monitor monthly fluctuations and, thereby, respond quickly to changes that do not follow proven sales cycles. Investigate the reason, and then make adjustments to meet demands. Focus on what sells. Drop what doesn't.

The example for completing Worksheet 5: Product Mix by Ratio to Sales has a corresponding blank in the back of the book. List the products by category. If the line is small you might want to list individual units as shown. An optional bar or line chart can be developed using spreadsheet software, such as Excel® or Lotus®.

SECTION THREE

III. THE MARKETPLACE: An Analysis
   1. Historical Background
   2. Emerging Trends
   3. Market Characteristics
   4. Pricing Trends
   5. Customer Considerations
   6. Supplier Considerations
   7. Competition

Section Three Objectives

This section provides your reader with a detailed description of the marketplace. More than any other section, it justifies your reason for being in business. Beginning with the Historical Information and working forward through, and including the Marketplace Summary, the plan is laid out in the following sequence.

Business Plan Sequence

III. THE MARKET-PLACE: An Analysis 1. Historical Background	Breakout of Industry Growth	2. Emerging Trends	Breakout of Trends Analysis	3. Market Characteristics	Breakout of Characteristics
Consumer Profile Data	4. Pricing Trends	Breakout Industry Pricing Trends Analysis	Breakout Your Company's Pricing Trends Data	5. Customer Considerations	6. Supplier Considerations
7. Competition	Competitor Market Share Analysis	Marketplace Summary			

A marketing analysis is necessary to establish product credibility and, therefore, the viability of the company. These findings build your case, so to speak. Data must be verifiable and documented throughout with footnotes. If you obtain data from print media, look for the resource in the body of the text or on the charts, usually at the bottom of the chart or sometimes at the end of the article. Contact the resource directly, double checking for accuracy. Always quote the resource, not the media where the data was obtained.

III. THE MARKETPLACE: AN ANALYSIS
1. Historical Background

Writer's Checklist:

- Briefly explain your industry and its unique aspects, if any.
- Demonstrate your industry's past strengths and future potential.
- Use bar charts (optional) to show industry growth over the past three/five years and project its growth over the same period.
- Use only data from recognized sources, such as government statistics or qualified studies from reliable organizations.

SAMPLE TEXT

Historical Background

The demand for software packaging closures is a worldwide industry representing $xx billion in sales this past year, Figure x, by breakout of major country markets. Overall, the industry had an annual grown rate of xx percent in the past five years, Figure xx, in spite of many setbacks relating to international labor laws, strikes, and restricting software distribution within certain countries. Allowing for inflation, industry growth is projected at a vigorous mean of xx percent a year over the next five years, Figure xxx.

This section briefly explains your industry's history, presenting any unique aspects. Use optional pie or bar charts to demonstrate its past strengths as well as future potential. The sample text in this instance, uses three different Figures to visually illustrate the information presented in the text. Show industry sales for the past five years and allowing for inflation, project industry sales for the next five years. If the industry has had setbacks and overcome them, or is on the road to recovery, explain this as a strength versus a weakness. Worksheet 6: Industry Growth, and Worksheet 7: Industry Overview, illustrate how the information is developed. Corresponding blanks are in the back of the book.

WORKSHEET 6: Industry Growth

Past	5 Years	% Growth	Projected	5 Years	% Growth
1996	$ xxx	15 %	2001	$ xxx	22 %
1997	$ xxx	13 %	2002	$ xxx	25 %
1998	$ xxx	15 %	2003	$ xxx	27 %
1999	$ xxx	17 %	2004	$ xxx	29 %
2000	$ xxx	20 %	2005	$ xxx	30%

WORKSHEET 7: Industry Overview

My Industry: Packaging   **Standard Industrial Code (SIC):** 123

Product Line: Packaging Closures   **Sub-SIC:** 123.456

a. Major Assets
1. Convenient for mailing software
2. Protects the software
3. Sure Lock offers security
4. Custom design packaging

b. Liabilities
1. Not fail safe
2. Knock-off's are probable
3. Finding design talent for custom work
4. Resin availability for making product

Major Marketing Regions

USA, Asia, Europe (breaking into Australia)

Industry (Major points, strengths, general comment's:

Security on software packaging is becoming increasingly
popular. Licensing our patent on the Sure Lock can be
very profitable. Need to speak to our attorney about this.

Most data is available from government resources, such as the *U.S. Industry and Trade Outlook.* This publication offers concise yet detailed analysis for almost all industries and is available through libraries or you may purchase the book for about $70. To place an order, call 800-553-6847 or send an email to *<orders@ntis.fedworld.gov>*. Another valuable resource is the *Statistical Abstract of the United States.* Published annually by the U.S. Department of Commerce, Bureau of the Census, it too, is available at most libraries. For more information call the Bureau at 301-457-4714.

There are situations, however, where applicable data is not available. For instance, if the product, service, or industry is new to your geographic region or is too small to be listed under its own Standard Industrial Code (SIC), it may be difficult to find information. Demographics may also be hard to obtain in emerging or Third World countries. If this is the case, there are a number of things you can do.

Depending on your budget, you can hire a marketing research firm or other professionals to collect customized data. You can also develop your own study criteria and collect this data yourself. Though not as reliable, you might use data from a broad category in which your product or service is a part and then draw conclusions regarding your venture. If you use a broad category, provide an explanation in the text.

Industry trade associations, related publications, and metro newspapers, also conduct surveys and develop highly detailed analysis on a variety of industries and topics. Large city and university libraries are invaluable for helping people identify and retrieve this data. You can also contact professional associations directly. The Internet also offers a wealth of data worldwide as described in Chapter One. Information is likewise available from local, regional, and state planning departments, and an assortment of government agencies or online subscriber databases.

Research data shouldn't be photocopied, as is, and then placed in your business plan instead of original text, charts, and figures. The same is true of articles clipped from publications.

2. Emerging Trends

Writer's Checklist

• Briefly describe industry trends that directly affect your business. This would include, yet not be limited to, the following:
- shifts in consumer preferences;
- shifts in user demographics;
- new technology utilization, e.g.: eCommerce
- new markets;
- skilled labor shortages;
- communication technologies, e.g.: wireless or streaming media

- Show trends on charts or graphs if this makes it easier and faster for the reader to understand the information.
- Explain findings in one or two paragraphs.

SAMPLE TEXT

Emerging Trends

The security packaging industry has seen substantial growth in the last three years as the software market expands to include Internet suppliers and vendors. This segment of the industry, Figure x, has grown by xx percent a year outpacing all other types of software packaging by xx percent. Leading edge research and development, together with new manufacturing technologies, are creating better resins for less cost while providing greater user benefits. For instance, closures are lighter in weight, but stronger than ever thought possible. Computer-aided design (CAD), too, when combined with Internet technologies, is shaping the way we deliver product today.

Since markets are in constant flux, use this section to address these changes. Studies, show that during any ten-year period, 98 percent of any market will completely reinvent itself. For instance, people move, are born, die, age, divorce, or marry. Fads come and go. Cultures and lifestyles change. Unforeseen economic and political developments impact the business climate. Wealth shifts from one sector to another. This, together with improved technologies, new discoveries and an ever-changing workforce, influences all industries worldwide.

Worksheet 8: Emerging Trends, shows how to log collected data, making it easier to explain your findings in one or two paragraphs. More times than not, this data is easier to understand when illustrated on a bar or line chart. Provide explanatory notes which may be included either within the chart itself or on the following page entitled "Notes to Figure." If notes are on the figure itself, use a 10 point type and/or a footnote. Write the word "Notes:" preceding the brief explanation.

3. Market Characteristics

Writer's Checklist

- Demonstrate user/market demographics and characteristics.
- Show product consumption.
- Provide median expenditures per capita by breakout of product type.
- Rank products or services by user preference.
- Use optional charts to illustrate characteristics.

WORKSHEET 8: Emerging Trends

Emerging Trends	Major Trend	Use of Application	Secondary Trend
User preferences:	Pilfer-resistant	mailers	Retail: single disks
User demographics:	See Worksheet 9	End-user direct	Not Applicable
New technologies:	Resins	Packaging closures	Seamless lightweight packaging
New markets:	Australia	Same as USA	Emerging countries
Labor	Sub-contract design	Telecommuters Saves $$	Multicultural
Communication:	3-D Software	Intranet/ Extranet	WebTV & wireless
Internet:	eCommerce	Demos & training	Streaming media

SAMPLE TEXT

Market Characteristics

The most popular software packaging closures weigh less than one-quarter of an ounce. Of these, the security closure is leading sales among buyers for industrial software packaging followed by buyers for redistributed training and development software, Figure x. Remarkably, the latter group makes xx percent of their purchases via the Internet using pre-approved credit transactions. Annual sales for the security lock are $xx billion, representing xx percent of the packaging industry's sales.

Now that your industry's background is established and emerging trends identified, describe its market characteristics, particularly product consumption patterns. The sample text illustrates what might be included. Use Worksheet 9: User/Buyer Characteristics, to develop your research. If you sell consumer goods, use Worksheet 10: Consumer Profiles. Blank worksheets for both are found in the back of the book. This data too, can be exhibited as a chart. Be as thorough and accurate as possible, since it is very important to understand the markets your company targets.

WORKSHEET 9: User/Buyer Characteristics

User/Buyer Type	Percent have Website	$ Median Annual Expenditures	Rate of Consumption
Industrial Software Developers	98%	$xxxxxxxx	Reorder Quarterly
Training & Development Redistribution	75%	$xxxxxxxx	Reorder Annually
Internet & Commercial Developers	100%	$xxxxxxxx	Reorder in 6 months

4. Pricing Trends

Writer's Checklist

- Show past and current industry pricing trends.
- Allow for inflation.
- Note any price variances, such as, labor costs in different regions, shipping, duties for different countries, taxes, etc.
- Project anticipated pricing trends over the short- to long-term, if applicable.
- Briefly explain pricing advantages or disadvantages.

SAMPLE TEXT

Pricing Trends

As shown in Figure xx, the price for software packaging closures has steadily declined since its introduction in the late 1980s. Note, however, how the product evolved in the same period, Figure xx. Features now include a multitude of designs. This has expanded product lines industrywide offering customers a wide variety of choices and prices. New technologies, as discussed in Section Two, Emerging Trends, promise to give customers an even greater choice of features and prices.

If applicable, show the past and current pricing trends by product mix. Allow for inflation. Note any price variances, such as, labor costs in different regions, shipping, duties for different countries, and taxes, if these affect your company.

Briefly explain pricing advantages or disadvantages. For instance, when hand held electronic calculators were introduced to the marketplace in the 1970s they were sold for approximately $500 each. In less than 10 years, the price had fallen as low as $8. Today, inexpensive models are given away as promotional enticements. The price drop could work to a retailer's advantage, since more consumers can afford to spend $8 than $500.

A calculator manufacturer, on the other hand, might view the price drop differently. First, the price drop clearly indicates that the market has become saturated with too many calculators. If the manufacturer is smart it will turn what appears to be a disadvantage into an advantage. The company could develop a highly competitive, yet innovative, calculator within a popular price range. In another scenario, an exporter might find new, viable markets for inexpensive calculators. These same analogies are true for almost all business situations.

Again, it is optional if you want to use a chart to illustrate industry pricing trends. Nearly all charts and graphs, by the way, can easily be displayed on a half-page. Some can fit side by side on a half-page as well. They should be large enough to make a statement, but not overwhelm the business plan format. Worksheet 11: Industry Pricing Trends, in the back of the book provides space for collecting this data. Show pricing trends for the past five years and project trends for the next three to five years.

5. Customer Considerations

Writer's Checklist

- Describe how customers are serviced.
- Describe what customers will be offered. This could be anything from free delivery to free customer support services.

SAMPLE TEXT

Customer Considerations

The software packaging industry has always provided customer support. This is a free service with the added courtesy of a toll free 800 number. Rising operational and payroll costs, however, have generated a trend whereby the customer pays for the telephone call.

Over the past six years multimedia tutorials have begun offering yet another level of customer support. Now, the popularity and massive expansion of the Internet is laying the groundwork for a major shift in the way software developers distribute products to their customers altogether. This is expected to alter current practices within the software packaging industry and increase annual sales for certain types of packaging by as much as xx percent over the next five years.

Customers are fickle, therefore, services must constantly change not only within your industry, but your business. With an objective eye toward the data gathered thus far, pinpoint at least three trends in your industry that could attract new customers simply because of unique or better service. This is a good time to pull your team together for an afternoon and explore all plausible ideas. Worksheet 12: Customer

Services, found in the back of the book, can be converted into a transparency and projected on a screen to facilitate discussions. Your team may emerge with surprisingly simple and easy-to-implement "why-didn't-we-think-of-this-sooner" ideas.

If you don't already, this may be a good time to begin the practice of monitoring monthly sales and flagging negative shifts in the market. Shifts, however, may not be customer related but rather influenced from an outside source, such as, the overall economy. If customer related, immediately nip the decline in the bud by querying customers directly to identify the problem. Results most always expose what is needed to reverse the trend.

6. Supplier Considerations

Writer's Checklist

- Address supplier-side problems, such as, labor shortages, import issues, technical, personnel, anything that could stall the delivery of your product or service.
- Discuss cost, if applicable.
- Define any special considerations.

SAMPLE TEXT

Supplier Considerations

ISO9000 is a globally recognized certificate of quality assurance suppliers. Original equipment manufacturers (OEM) and prime contractors worldwide are faced with the same problem, finding certified ISO9000 companies. Studies have shown that using non-certified contractors can add as much as 7 percent to end user costs. To help its members, the International Packaging Association joined forces with the Association of ISO9000 Companies to develop industry-specific training programs.

Every industry has supplier concerns. Outline the most important ones in your plan and provide solutions to potential problems. Worksheet 13: Supplier Considerations, will help flush out ideas. When you have competed the worksheet, briefly state the problem and a solution in just one paragraph or no more than two.

Incidentally, there isn't any need to mention suppliers by name or provide a supplier-list since plans can inadvertently fall into the wrong hands. A business plan doesn't have to provide such detail as to help your competitors or anyone, for that matter, discover your trade secrets and a ready made blueprint for competing against you.

WORKSHEET 13: Supplier Characteristics

Disadvantages	Probable Solutions
Finding ISO9000 Certified suppliers	Join with other companies in the area to train suppliers. Are there any tax advantages (ask accountant)?
Limited resin suppliers with major one in the North. Presents a winter shipping problem.	Purchase a four-month supply of resin for Nov. 1 through March 1. Need to check with purchasing for what we need.

Advantages	Value Added
Subcontracting work. Industry is known for its co-marketing efforts.	No overhead burden during down cycle. Stretches marketing dollars while providing additional sales opportunities that otherwise might not have developed.

Throughout your plan, meet concerns and obstacles head on. If plausible, turn concerns into opportunities; if not, define any barriers and describe an alternate course of action. Disclosing any probable setbacks with accompanying solutions lends credibility to a business plan.

7. Competition

Writer's Checklist

- Identify major competitors by name.
- Briefly describe competitors' advertising and promotional activities.
- Show competitors market share, if possible, using a bar chart.

SAMPLE TEXT

Competition

There are 20 major competitors in the USA, Asia, Europe, and Australia as shown in Figure xx by breakout of market share. Seven competitors share xx percent of the market while xx percent for the market is shared among 12 small companies with NyTec having 2 percent. Market share is further detailed in the Marketing Planning chapter that follows.

Identify your competitors by name and, if possible, breakout the percentage of market share for each. It also helps to briefly describe your competitors' sales and advertising tactics. Keeping an eye on competition is key to survival and the more you know, the better you can plan. Worksheet 14: Competition, in the back of the book, is useful in pulling this data together.

The Web not withstanding, collecting competitive data is sometimes difficult — another reason to join an industry trade association. If you find getting information is a problem, speak directly with competitors, suppliers, and customers. Other ways to collect competitive data include the following:

- Prior to opening a retail store, walk or drive around a 10-block radius of the planned location. Shop the competition. Make notes regarding the display of merchandise, inventory selections, overall decor, attitudes toward customers, prices, cleanliness, and more. Would you shop there? If not, why? Since 80 percent of a retailer's customers come from within a five-mile radius, locate competitors on a map. Will the market support your store as well? Do competitors have websites? If so, how are they using the Web?

- If you are a distributor, call buyers directly to identify competitors. Ask buyers what they like and don't like about distributors. Discover what they want and need. This information can later be used in the marketing planning section of your plan. If competitive data for distributors are not available, use product sales data from your industry research. Then, estimate the quantities your buyers most likely purchase and from whom. How can you service customers over the Web better than other distributors?

- Annual reports can be very helpful if you are a manufacturer, particularly if your competitors are public companies. Reliable data for niche markets is not as easy to find. Take advantage of the vast databases on the Internet, and query distributors, reps, and buyers alike.

This chapter of the plan is one of the most important, as mentioned earlier. It must prove your market exists. Everything from this point forward will pivot on these findings. You are encouraged to use charts and graphs at every turn, as they are quick and easy to understand.

When marketing research is woven together, it exposes almost everything you need to know about your industry, its marketplace, competitors, and customers. Now, eCommerce has added another facet. Without good research, marketing planning is next to impossible. Investors, too, depend on this section of a business plan to help them form an opinion about the industry and how your company will play out in it.

Again, a chapter summary isn't a prerequisite; however, it can accomplish a number of things. As the following summary reveals, it zeroes in on major points, providing readers with a quick overview and setting the stage for the next chapter.

OPTIONAL SAMPLE TEXT

Marketing Analysis Summary

Historically, the software packaging industry has shown a steady growth of xx percent a year over the past five years. An average projected annual growth rate of xx percent is expected over the next five years, adjusting for inflation and the introduction of eCommerce. Although the industry is growing, not all products are expected to grow with it. For example, the slip closures are showing signs of market saturation, while the snap fastener closures are selling at two times the overall industry growth rate.

Globally, the industry is gaining in popularity, particularly in Germany, France, Japan, and Australia with a combined market size of xxxxx commercial and institutional users. Industrywide, commercial sales account for $xx billion annually, institutional $xx billion.

The average size of an order for industrial software packaging is estimated at $xxx. The average expenditure, collectively, is $xxx annually. Industry pricing trends are keeping pace with inflation with modest price increases annually, but not in all product categories. Products on a downward sales cycle are decreasing in price by just under 30 percent. NyTec's market share is estimated a xx percent.

Writing the Business Plan

SECTION FOUR

IV. MARKETING PLANNING
 1. Market Segments
 2. eBusiness
 3. Distribution Channels
 4. Pricing Policies
 5. Market Share
 6. Sales Plan
 7. Advertising Plan
 8. Public Relations

Section Four Objectives

The marketing planning section is the most important in the plan. Based on your marketing analysis, it establishes sales goals and creates a competitive marketing strategy with budgets. It includes eight different topics and is laid out in the following sequence.

Business Plan Sequence

IV. MARKETING PLANNING 1. Market Segments	Market Segment Matrix	2. eBusiness	Breakout of Website Content	3. Distribution Channels	Chart of Distribution Channels
4. Pricing Policies	5. Market Share	6. Sales Plan	Marketing Projections Chart	Tactical Marketing Path (Summary)	7. Advertising Plan

Business Plan Sequence, continued

Advertising Schedule and Budget	8. Public Relations	Public Relations Schedule and Budget	Marketing Plan Summary

With the explosion of eCommerce, marketing planning means wearing an exciting new hat. Key words to plan against are fast, custom, direct, global, discount, and the best words of all, "immediate cash flow" if you are selling directly to end-users. The king of eCommerce, Cisco Systems, Inc. *<www.cisco.com>*, now generates $12+ million in sales per day over the Internet. There are over a million websites selling products, with the average small business generating over $600,000 annually.

IV. MARKETING PLANNING
1. Market Segments

Writer's Checklist

- Define market segments by products sold to each segment.
- Use an optional chart to clarify information.
- Refer back to previous sections, as needed, to support your marketing rationale. Not only will this provide continuity for the reader, it will justify your marketing decisions.

SAMPLE TEXT

Market Segments

As noted in Chapter II, Product Mix by Ratio to Sales, page x, NyTec produces closures and creates custom design software packaging. Markets are divided into four segments: industrial software developers, training and development buyers who redistribute software, commercial, and Internet software developers. Overall there are xxx potential customers in NyTec's international sales territory who meet its criteria.

Markets are segmented to produce the greatest sales potential. Niche markets also exist within segmented markets. In NyTec's case this might mean the company would only want to reach and sell those customers with annual sales over $10 million that have purchased a specific software packaging product within the last

---

WORKSHEET 15: Market Segments

Market Segment — Niche	Product Mix			
	Sure Lock Mailers	Sure Lock Disk Storage	Easy Close Envelope Slip	Easy Close Slip & Snap
1. Industrial Software	X	X	X	X
2. Training Software Redistribution, Corps & Training Companies	x			x
3. Commercial Developers	x	x	x	x
4. Internet, Free Promotions and Mailers	x		x	

---

year. Worksheet 15: Market Segments illustrates how NyTec defined their market segments. A blank worksheet is provided in the back of the book.

2. eBusiness

Writer's Checklist

• Highlight your eCommerce marketing plans for conducting eBusiness.
• Address a timeline for integrating conventional and virtual markets.

SAMPLE TEXT

eBusiness

NyTec is currently integrating its traditional marketing activities with the Internet. Website development for Phase I, is complete. Phase II and III will follow within the next three to five months. Web sales are expected to overtake conventional sales channels over the next two years, Figure xx, Internet Marketing Timeline, and expand NyTec's marketing arena worldwide.

Typically, communications and marketing activities on the Web fall within these three categories: a public access area, an Extranet, and Intranet (See Figure 4.1). Public access accommodates requests from your customers and the general public. The requested information is not confidential and open to anyone who might visit your site. An Extranet accommodates business associates and customers who are external to your organization, such as purchasing agents, suppliers, or customers who register their product warranties. Extranets are typically behind firewalls and

FIGURE 4.1

PUBLIC ACCESS Typical Requests	EXTRANET Typical Requests	INTRANET Typical Needs
Customers and Public	Buyers, Suppliers, and Customers	Internal and Field Personnel
Information	New Product Information	Marketing Research
Order Placement	Price Changes	Company Announcements
Newsletters—Media	Schematics	Training
Catalogs, Brochures	General Announcements	Sales Department
Employment	Instruction	Project Updates
General Query	Ordering	Internal Recruitment

WORKSHEET 16: Extranet and Intranet

	No. Pgs.	Internal No. Users	External No. Users
Extranet: Customer			
User Instructions	2	1 User, Updates only	Unknown
Warranty Registration	1	Automated	Unknown
Product Warranties	1	Not Applicable	Not applicable
Marketing Surveys	1	1 User, Automated	Unknown
Extranet: Suppliers			
Price Lists	4	1 User	25 includes sales reps
Price Changes	n/a	1 User, Updates only	Not applicable
Schematics	Varies	5 Users	25
Intranet			
Team Projects	Varies	24 employees	Sales reps/12 users
Training Programs	50	27 employees	25
Policies Manual	17	All employees	25
Marketing Research	300+	2 in Marketing dept.	Not applicable
Sales Department	Varies	14	Sales reps/12 users

users are given individual pin numbers known as "permissions" to access the area. Intranets, discussed earlier, house internal data and are off limits to the public or outside associates. Some Extranets and Intranets are housed on separate servers connected to the Internet; many use both filter software and server-based firewalls.

Your website can drastically reduce many of the operational costs traditionally associated with these business functions. In turn, this influences end-user prices by providing an improved use of time and customer courtesies, thereby, reducing overhead. Worksheet 16: Extranet and Intranet, and its companion Worksheet 17: Website Contents, were developed to help you create a timeline and identify company requirements. These worksheets along with Worksheet 3: Business Information, which you completed from Section One, will form the structure for the content of your website. The preceding sample text illustrates how you might combine this information and present it in your business plan.

3. Distribution Channels

Writer's Checklist

- If your goods or services move from you to the end-user, like NyTec's, explain the process in a few sentences or a few paragraphs.
- Multiple distribution channels should be displayed on a chart (see Figure 4.2). A fictitious company, other than NyTec, was used to show how goods can move from one place to the next on their way to an end-user.

SAMPLE TEXT

Direct to End-User

Discussed throughout this plan, NyTec distributes its products directly to end-users. The closures are attached to the software packaging per the customer's specifications.

SAMPLE TEXT

Multiple Distribution Channels

High End Art, Ltd., has marketed its products using three conventional sales methods with eight different distribution channels for the last five years, Figure xx. Over the next six months, the Internet will be integrated into High End Art's in-house sales department adding the ninth marketing and distributional channel.

WORKSHEET 17: Website Content

Content	Phases* I	II	III	Firewall Yes	No	Developmental Ideas and Comments
Extranet: Customer						
User Instructions	x			x		
Warranty Registration	x			x		Link to marketing research
Product Warranties	x				x	
Extranet: Suppliers						
Price Lists	x			x		Updates as needed
Price Changes	x			x		
Schematics	x			x		
Intranet						
Team Projects and Updates		x		x		Constantly changing
Employee Training				x		Review vendors
Policies Manual	x		x	x		programs
Marketing Research		x		x		
Marketing Surveys	x			x		Tie into ongoing plan
Public Access						
Events and Demos		x			x	Keep updated
Company Background	x					
Annual Report			x			
Co. Email/Tel Directory	x					
Employee Vita and Photo		x				
Job Openings	x					
Newsletter			x			
Customer Services	x					
Single Product Flyers	x					
Catalog with 15 Products	x					
Order Forms	x					
Media Releases			x			

* Determine Phase Timelines: Phase I: <u>March 1</u>   Phase II: <u>July 1</u>   Phase III: <u>October 1</u>

FIGURE 4.2: **Multiple Distribution Channels**

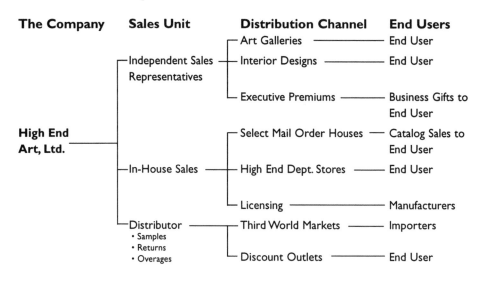

The Company	Sales Unit	Distribution Channel	End Users

High End Art, Ltd.

Independent Sales Representatives
- Art Galleries — End User
- Interior Designs — End User
- Executive Premiums — Business Gifts to End User

In-House Sales
- Select Mail Order Houses — Catalog Sales to End User
- High End Dept. Stores — End User
- Licensing — Manufacturers

Distributor
- Samples
- Returns
- Overages
- Third World Markets — Importers
- Discount Outlets — End User

FIGURE 4.3

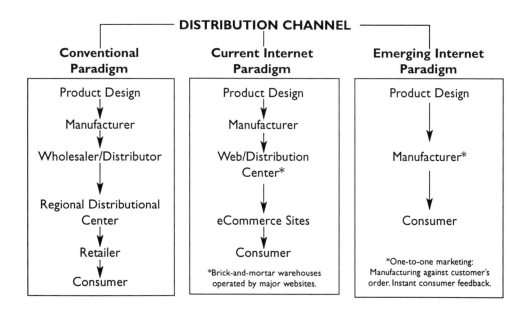

DISTRIBUTION CHANNEL

Conventional Paradigm

Product Design
↓
Manufacturer
↓
Wholesaler/Distributor
↓
Regional Distributional Center
↓
Retailer
↓
Consumer

Current Internet Paradigm

Product Design
↓
Manufacturer
↓
Web/Distribution Center*
↓
eCommerce Sites
↓
Consumer

*Brick-and-mortar warehouses operated by major websites.

Emerging Internet Paradigm

Product Design
↓
Manufacturer*
↓
Consumer

*One-to-one marketing: Manufacturing against customer's order. Instant consumer feedback.

eCommerce is changing distributional channels causing suppliers to shift from mass merchandising to one-to-one marketing, as shown in Figure 4.3. In the current and emerging paradigms, providers are moved closer to end-users. Companies such as Dell computers are proving it is both possible and more profitable to identify, track, individually service, satisfy, maintain, and resell existing customers one at a time versus accumulating more customers, though not to an exclusion.

Change, though, takes time. Major e-tailers like Amazon.com, eBay and others have had to rethink the idea of drop-shipping products from the original manufacturer directly to end-users and open their own warehouses. What seemed like a revolutionary distributional approach in the early days of the Net, didn't take into consideration the majority of manufacturers were not prepared to ship orders one at a time to individuals. Entrenched in yesterday's business model, these manufacturers are invested heavily in sophisticated inventory systems for bulk shipments to distributional center warehouses. To accommodate shipments to individual consumers, manufactures will have to redesign their entire systems, which is a costly process. If you are planning to e-tail product, contact the manufacturer *before* you make any decisions about how you will distribute product in the world of "click and mortar."

Worksheet 18: Distribution Channels, is provided in the back of the book to develop a channel appropriate for your type of business.

4. Pricing Policies

Writer's Checklist

- Briefly describe your company's pricing policies.
- Explain the different pricing tiers.
- If applicable, make a competitive price comparison.

SAMPLE TEXT

Pricing Policies

NyTec has four pricing tiers consisting of the following:

- Small Runs
- Quantity Price Breaks
- Group Sales
- Nonprofit and Charity

For industrywide software packaging details, please refer to Pricing Trends and Competition in Chapter Three. NyTec's prices are highlighted in Appendix xx.

This section of the marketing plan explains your pricing policies as they relate to prices within your industry as well as to your major competitors. Many companies have different pricing tiers as illustrated in the sample text. Provide sensitive information, such as price lists, to serious investors under separate cover. Worksheet

19: Pricing Policies, will help sort out your pricing structure if you don't have one.

5. Market Share

Writers Checklist

• Qualify your market share by referencing research found elsewhere in the plan.
• If a bar chart was originally used to illustrate your competitors' market share in Chapter Three, add your data to the same chart. Copy it and include it here.

SAMPLE TEXT

Market Share

As discussed in the previous chapter, NyTec has 20 major competitors in the USA, Asia, Europe, and Australia. Seven competitors share xx percent of the market while xx percent for the market is shared among 12 small companies with NyTec having a xx percent share. With the introduction of its patented Sure Lock, NyTec's market share is projected to increase to xx percent over the next two years. This includes Internet sales.

Market share has always been key to a company's core strategy. In virtual marketing, however, projecting market share becomes more difficult for most industries. For instance, it is rather easy to identify how market shares breakout for Internet service providers and online services. But what about the candlestick maker? Virtual marketing software can help the company track its candlestick orders from around the globe, but can it help managers estimate market share? With difficulty.

Most companies will have to be content projecting conventional market share while rethinking virtual sales projections. There is no foreseeable formula, as sales over the Internet are sporadic and global versus consistent and geographically specific. However, the Web offers an ideal delivery system for one-to-one marketing since Internet sales are highly individualized from product to product, from website to website, and from company to company.

6. Sales Plan

Writer's Checklist

• Tie your plan together with three- to five-year sales projections.
• Support all of the data presented in the plan.
• Present an overview of your tactical approach.
• Establish sales goals.

• Is the plan financially feasible?

```
SAMPLE TEXT
```

Sales Plan

NyTec's five-year sales projections, Figure xx, show an overall increase from $xx million in gross sales in year one to $xx million in year five by breakout of product mix. Account retention and acquisition for each year, as well as the number of employees needed to meet these projections are also shown. Explanatory notes follow the Figure.

Business plans require sales projections, but providing details are unnecessary. For instance, the Sure Lock product is projected over a five-year period. In the first year there are no accounts since the product is new. The goal is to acquire 30 accounts over a 12-month period for a combined value of $xx thousand — or a $xx mean value per account. The company begins Year Two with 30 existing accounts, but in Year Two must allow for account loss. The Easy Close represents $xx million in Year One, but is expected to experience a sales decline in each of the five years. Worksheet 20: The Five-Year Sales Projection Chart, shows how to develop a one-page format for projecting sales covering a five-year period. This format will work for any business and almost all industries.

Anyone viewing this chart can rapidly determine whether a company's sales objectives are practical or not. Too, these projections are tied to financial statements covering the same five-year period. It is simple for a reader to critique your overall rationale. All the reader has to do is examine the Executive Summary, the Marketing Analysis Summary, the Five-Year Sales Projections Chart, and then look through the financial statements. The rationale is quickly borne out in about 10 minutes. This is extremely appealing to bankers or investors — as well as to your managers. Everyone is going in the same direction with a synergistic tailwind. Keep text concise and simple, letting the charts in this section sell your story. Add a "Notes" page following the sales chart explaining how projections were developed. The same product mix used makes up the revenue list in the financial statements.

Instructions for Worksheet 20: Five-Year Sales Projections Chart

Product Mix: Breakout your product mix as illustrated. NyTec only has two groups of products, the Sure Lock and Easy Close. There are different styles in each, however (Worksheet 5).

Years: Number the years from one to five. This is particularly handy for a proposed

WORKSHEET 20: Five-Year Sales Projections

Product Mix	Year	Annual Gross (millions)								# Existing Accounts	# New Accounts	Projected Annual Gross
		.25	.50	1.0	2.0	3.0	4.0	5.0	6.0			
Sure Lock	1									0	30	$xxx
	2									25	40	xxx
	3									65		xxx
	4											xxx
	5											xxx
Easy Close	1											
	2											
	3											
	4											
	5											

NyTec had 30 new accounts in year-one, but five were one-time accounts. Therefore, it started the year with 25 accounts and acquired 40 new accounts to start year-three with 65 accounts. Always allow for account loss.

Add as many products or services as you need.

	Yr. 1	Yr. 2	Yr. 3	Yr. 4	Yr. 5
Combined Annual Gross	$xxx	$xxx	$xxx	$xxx	$xxx
Number of Employees	27	35	42	55	70

company since year one will not start until funding and other activities are underway. Use the calendar or fiscal year if your company is established and sales are already in progress.

Annual Gross (Bar Chart): Adjust the annual/gross currency to suit your business. Selecting a distinct color or gray shade to correspond with each year makes the bar chart easier to read. Repeat the five-year bar chart for each product mix.

Number of Existing Accounts: Allow for account loss during a given year. Use actual records. If you are describing a proposed company, estimate losses between 10 and 15 percent. Show projections for each year for each group of products. This is a forerunner to developing detailed sales goals and tactics.

Number of New Accounts: Project account acquisitions from market share. This may mean obtaining so many retail stores, wholesale accounts, individual clients, or so many contracts. Use a median product or account value to estimate totals. For instance, one retail account might have ten stores, with each store buying 50 units for a value of $xx per account. Or, one new business client represents a median of value of $xx.

Project Annual Gross: Project the total gross sales for each year. Financial projections cannot be prepared without marketing projections. They mirror each other.

Combined Annual Gross: Add the sales from each product mix for Year One to determine the first year's sales total. Repeat for each subsequent year.

Number of Employees: Using realistic estimates of time use and management, project the number of employees needed to achieve company goals.

Developing an Integrated Tactical Marketing Path

The Integrated Tactical Marketing Path was redressed and renamed for *businessplan.com*. The underlying idea was originally created by David C. Karlson, Ph.D., an author and former Dean, Continuing Education Department, University of Maryland. Many times the words "sales" and "marketing" are incorrectly used as synonyms. Marketing is an entire process whereas, sales is just one part of that process. Creating an Integrated Tactical Marketing Path produces sales, but only as the end result of very specific decisions and actions.

Integration, in this instance, means the complementary blending of all marketing activities, including Internet strategies. "Tactical," which was coined as a catch-word by marketers some years ago, is a military term meaning the science of maneuvering forces in combat and the skill of using available means to reach an end — a perfect word here, since marketing has become an exacting science. We create strategies to move our forces to compete for customers or clients with available means — innovation, know-how, personnel, and money — to reach year-end sales goals.

The two-page tactical worksheets are meant to help you produce very clear and definite plans. At a glance they appear easy enough to complete, yet you will find that this tactical marketing path is a challenging and effective tool for fine-tuning your ideas.

Use one two-page worksheet for *each* tactic. When completed, only include your tactical summaries in the sales text of the business plan. Don't include confidential tactical worksheets in business plans.

Before you begin creating your tactical marketing plan, establish overall company goals, objectives, and tactical approaches. Goals and objectives are sometimes confused. To clarify, NyTec's *goal* is to provide customers with award winning custom software packaging designs that use the Easy Close and Sure Lock closures. NyTec's *objectives* include expanding their market to Australia, launching their patented closure, and completing their website to conduct eCommerce. *Tactics* include reaching all their markets with an advertising campaign in trade publications, directories, and the Yellow Pages; hosting free seminars that add job-related value to NyTec's customers, sales calls, monthly newsletter and design review, and approval and sales over the Internet. A company may have as many objectives as it can financially sustain.

7. Advertising Plan: Traditional and Virtual

Writer's Checklist

- Plan ad campaigns to coincide with the timing of major sales activities and annual business cycles.
- Provide a schedule and budget for the campaign.
- List selected advertising media by category, name and cost.
- Integrate Web advertising into your plan.

SAMPLE TEXT

Advertising Plan

NyTec has allocated xx percent of gross sales for advertising in the next fiscal year. The company has budgeted an additional xx percent of projected gross for its new website sales catalog, for a combined annual advertising budget total of $xxx. The monthly advertising budget and schedule escalate in February, September, and December following the company's seasonal sales cycle (see Figure xx, Advertising Schedule and Budget).

The company's innovative online ordering form captures the customer's profile, which is maintained on NyTec's database and updated accordingly. When new products are matched to this profile, an automatic notice is immediately emailed to the cus-

WORKSHEET 21: Integrated Tactical Marketing Path

NT Integrated Tactical Marketing Path Activities
(Use one worksheet for each tactic. Confidential—For Internal Use Only.)

Tactical Title: Introduce NyTec in Australia thru an Internet-Based Training Program

Contact Team and Numbers: T. Williams, Team Lead, (123) 456-7890

Objectives: Acquire three major corporate and six training accounts over the next 12 months in Australia, for a combined total of nine accounts with a mean average of $xxx in monthly sales.

Tactic: Webcast introductory packaging design training over our website 24-hours a day. Invite prospects from specific newsgroups to attend. Capture their names and contact numbers from required registration. Tie to print media campaign.

Market Segment for This Tactic: All packaging and design, corporate trainers, and purchasing agents newsgroups (hopefully) in Australia.

Three Client-Buying Considerations:
1. An immediate email acknowledgment to those who register for the training.
2. Training is free.
3. Our training provides another level of support in our industry.

Competitors' Use of This Tactic: None presently, however, 65 percent of the competitors now have websites. We need to hit the marketplace fast with email and follow-up calls to optimize our potential customer-conversion ratio.

Obstacles to This Tactic:

1. Capital needed to cover and ride out investment through the sales process to cash flow.

2. Finding personnel with computer skill levels to meet ongoing needs.

3. Ongoing investment in maintaining website and updating software annually.

4. Developing solid relationships with our sales team.

WORKSHEET 21: Integrated Tactical Marketing Path, continued

Action Plan	Timeline	Deadline	Persons
1. Complete webcasting training package	3 wks.	6/27	DK
2. Identify list of newsgroups	2 wks.	6/20	PL
3. Create direct mailing piece for follow-up	4 wks.	7/7	MB
4. Complete software development	5 wks	7/14	RS & VC
5. Prep newsgroup posting	1 wk.	7/21	All
6. Post direct mail inf. on website	2 wks.	7/21	DK
7. Coordinate tactic with ad campaign	4 wks	7/22	MB
8. Launch		7/29	All

Success Milestones

Immediate: Contract with xx corp. and xx training firms within 3 months of launch.

6 Months: Contract with xx corp. and xx training firms in next 3-month period.

12 Months: Contract with xx corp. and xx training firms during following 6 months to reach year-end sales goals.

Action	Costs[*]	No. of Hours	Action	Costs	No. of Hours
1. Webcast	$ 4,000	200	5. Prep Posting	$2,000	20
2. ID List	$ 2,000	40	6. Mail	$3,000	80
3. Hardware	$21,000	N/A	8. Postage	$3,000 (estimated) (one-time cost)	

12-Month Use Frequency

Month
Jan (Feb) (Mar) Apr May Jun Jul Aug Sep Oct Nov Dec

Weeks
1(1)234 1(2)34 1(2)34 1234 1234 1234 1234 1234 1234 1234 1234 1234

Comments: Provide new training material for webcasting each week for two months, then rerun. If registration drops revise plans.

Total Hours: 340 hrs.   **Completion Date:** 7/29

Total Budget: $35,000   **Team Leader:** T. Williams, ext. 111

[*]Estimate costs based on the following: Annual salary, plus benefits, times 15 percent G&A = Cost

tomer, as well as designated newsgroups, with the company's URL in the message. Internet advertising will also be used in conjunction with conventional advertising in trade publications that offer a combination print and Web advertising package.

Many inexperienced entrepreneurs, as well as seasoned businesses, cut back on

---

FIGURE 4.4: Average Annual Advertising Expenditures as a Percent of Projected Gross Sales

Business Type	Average		
Amusement/Recreational Services	4.4 %	Gasoline Service Stations	0.8 %
Appliances/Electronics:		Gift and Novelty Stores	3.7
- Annual sales under $1 million	3.3	Hardware Stores	2.3
- $1 million to $10 million	2.8	Home Centers	1.9
- Over $10 million	3.9	Home Furnishings	5.4
Auto Accessories & Parts	0.9	Hotels & Motels	3.5
Auto Dealers	1.0	Insurance Agents and Brokers	0.8
Auto Repairs & Services	2.5	Jewelry Stores	6.2
Bakeries	1.8	Laundromats	1.2
Banks	1.3	Liquor Stores	0.9
Beauty Shops	2.0	Lumber Yards	0.8
Bicycle Dealers	2.0	Mail Order Houses	17.1
Book Stores	2.0	Meat Markets	0.6
Camera Stores	2.6	Men's Wear Stores	3.1
Catalog Showrooms	5.4	Motion Picture Theaters	4.1
Children's & Infants' Wear Stores	1.4	Music Stores	1.8
Cocktail Lounges	0.9	Nutritional Food Stores	3.0
Computer Stores	3.7	Office Furniture	0.7
Credit Institutions	1.6	Office Supply Dealers	1.3
Decorating Retailers	2.5	Ophthalmologists	5.0
Department Stores — Annual Sales:		Opticians	7.0
- $5 – $9.9 million	3.1	Pet Stores	3.7
- $10 – $19.9 million	4.1	Photographic Studios and Supplies	2.4
- $20 – $49.9 million	3.8	Real Estate	1.2
- $50 – $99.9 million	3.0	Restaurants	2.1
- Over $100 million	2.7	Savings and Loans	1.5
Discount Stores	2.4	Shoe Stores	2.0
Drug Store Chains	1.7	Specialty Stores	3.0
Drug Store Independents	1.1	Sporting Goods Stores	3.2
Dry Cleaners	2.3	Taverns	0.7
Educational Services	4.7	Tire Dealers	2.2
Florists	1.5	Travel Agents	5.0
Food Chains	1.3	Variety Stores	2.2
Furniture Stores	7.1		

advertising when the going gets tough. Others never allocate enough money for advertising. A new business, however, is like any other relationship. There is a getting acquainted period. It simply takes time to create demand and develop a loyal following. Advertising helps a business get established. Worksheets 22 through 24 in the back of the book can guide your planning process for advertising.

An advertising campaign mimics the peaks and valleys of a marketing plan and the budget is based on a percentage of projected annual gross sales. Allow for a much higher ad budget during the first 18 months of a new business. Developed from material supplied by *The Los Angeles Times*, Figure 4.4 lists the average expenditures for an assortment of industries. Since budgets vary widely, check with your industry association of the American Association of Advertising Agencies for specifics (*www.commercepart.com/AAAA/index.html*).

Before planning your campaign, inquire if your suppliers offer co-op advertising incentives. Co-op programs act like a partnership between the manufacturer, distributor or retailer adding dollars to an ad budget, and now with the Internet affiliate program, times are changing for the better. For additional information contact your newspaper or the Newspaper Advertising Co-Operative Network (NACON) through your library's directory resources.

Use Worksheet 25: 12-Month Advertising Schedule and Budget, to spell out where, when, and how advertising will coincide with major sales activities and your annual business cycles. During a 12-month period, increase your advertising during peak sales and hold the line in months that are traditionally slow. When projecting your annual budget, include all co-op advertising programs, directory listings, such as, the Yellow Pages, and other related costs charged off to the advertising department.

FIGURE 4.5: **Best Month for Mailings**

Business Type	J	F	M	A	M	J	J	A	S	O	N	D
Business/Finance	x		x				x		x			x
Cultural	x					x	x		x	x		x
Self Improvement	x	x						x	x			x
Home Interest	x	x					x		x			x
Parents and Children	x	x					x	x				x
Hobbies and Related	x						x		x			x
Entertainment	x						x		x			x
Education/Technical	x		x			x			x			x
Fund Raising	x	x	x						x	x	x	

Direct mail is still a valuable advertising tool, although it can become expensive. According to the Direct Marketing Association, New York, some months are better than others for direct mail campaigns depending upon the type of business (see Figure 4.5). The United States Postal Service also offers an excellent Direct Mail Delivers™ kit free, call 1-888-USPS, extension 2104.

No matter how carefully an ad campaign is planned, though, there are limits as to what advertising can and cannot do. For example:

It can
- Help establish your company's identity and image.
- Attract new customers and keep your name in front of existing customers.
- Stimulate sales.
- Distinguish you from competitors.
- Grow your business.

It cannot
- Solve pressing financial problems.
- Fool people into buying inferior products.
- Create loyalty among customers.
- Create an immediate and substantial upward turn in sales.
- Substitute for poor customer relations by creating the impression the company stands behind its products when clearly it won't.
- Substitute for overall poor management and lack of planning.

8. Public Relations

Writer's Checklist

- Identify causes for your company to support or champion.
- Create a media release theme and schedule.
- Public relations should be:
  - A complement to your overall marketing plan;
  - Timed to match your advertising plan; and
  - Consistent over the long-term.

SAMPLE TEXT

Public Relations

NyTec works closely with local schools to promote and encourage computer skills among students. For the past five years, the company has sponsored two major charitable fund-raisers, dividing the proceeds between the schools in each of its marketing areas. In this coming year, each employee will begin donating one hour per month to teach grade school children different uses for multimedia software. These and other civic-minded contributions complement NyTec's advertising campaign (see Figure xx, 12-Month Public Relations Schedule).

The best known elements of a public relations plan include writing media releases on a regular basis and giving keynote talks at business and trade meetings. More and more businesses, however, are recognizing the value of community service by encouraging managers to serve as board members for charitable organizations or by sponsoring fund-raisers for worthy nonprofits. A socially responsible company benefits from these and other philanthropic activities in a number of ways. Community involvement creates goodwill among the members of a company's buying public, adds to the prestige of a company's image, and keeps the name of the business in front of its market.

Contributing to the well being of a community sends a message to a company's potential market: "your patronage is appreciated." Good publicity has a greater influence over a market than advertising. As media relation professionals often point out, "Advertising is what you *pay* for, publicity what you *pray* for." Worksheet 26: Public Relations Ideas, and Worksheet 27: Public Relations Activities, will help coordinate your PR campaign. The same 12-month schedule and budget you used for advertising can be applied here. Worksheet 28: 12-Month Public Relations Schedule and Budget, is identical to the Advertising Schedule and Budget you just completed.

Marketing Plan Summary

The marketing planning section is the backbone of your business plan. Its strength must be practical yet aggressive, creating in your readers an excitement and confidence that your company can do what it claims — successfully. It must also show investors or lenders the merits of your plan without handing them the key to the front door. This may seem like a dichotomy, although it isn't. For instance, you might reveal that you distribute your goods or services through "x" number of outlets in a certain geographic area, but you're not providing customer lists. Or, you might describe how many unit sales are projected, but you're not providing a detailed tactical outline for achieving these sales goals. The following synopsis should be polished with the same care you give sales brochures.

OPTIONAL SAMPLE TEXT

Marketing Plan Summary

NyTec's five-year projections show sales growing from $xx million in Year One to approximately $xxx million in Year Five. This may appear ambitious, however, the company not only has developed strong customer relationships in the USA, Asia, and

Europe, the patent for the Sure Lock in these regions has already been approved. Too, plans are underway to open the Australian market within the next three months, further expanding NyTec's opportunities.

Within the next two to six months, the company will have expanded its website providing an added distributional channel. Web sales are expected to overtake conventional sales methods within two years. Excluding website activities, xx percent of projected gross has been allocated for conventional advertising in each of the five following years. This is in addition to a very active public relations and community service program.

The company anticipates capturing a 5 percent market share by Year Three following the introduction of its patented product line. Projected growth is steady in terms of units shipped while allowing for inflation. Of interest, however, is the positive spread in profits from Year One to Year Five. This is achieved through utilizing the Internet, Extranet, and Intranet to reduce operating costs by as much as 95 percent in some areas. In capsule, NyTec is now positioned to expand its markets and increase sales without the associated costs.

V. MANAGEMENT AND ORGANIZATION
1. Management
2. Advisory Board
3. Strategic Alliances
4. Staffing
5. Organization Structure

Section Five Objectives

This section focuses on the company's management team, including advisors, and their demonstrated ability to grow a business. It includes five different elements and is laid out in the following sequence.

Business Plan Sequence

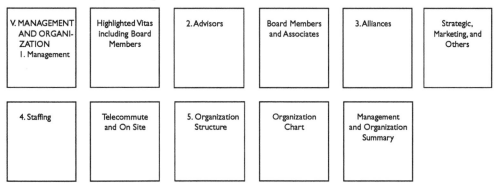

Entrepreneurs, key managers, and corporate executives usually enjoy writing this part of a business plan. There is a certain level of comfort in writing from experience. The ever-changing marketplace, however, presents executives with constant challenges.

Developing this section provides an opportunity to study what demands will be placed on your company's top team and advisors. Will they be able to leap over the limits of yesterday's business model and grasp the ring of today's prototype? Will you need a CSO, CTO, and a CIO? What changes will your CSO make in your SFA? What is a portal company? Why is company power shifting to the IS executive and what role can the CFO play that is different from a CPA? If answers to the questions have already been established, you are light years ahead of the rest. Answers are located at the end of this chapter on page 90, as well as addressed, in part, in this plan chapter.

V. MANAGEMENT AND ORGANIZATION
1. Management

Writer's Checklist

- Summarize your company's management philosophy and team in the first few sentences.
- Highlight the management team's positions in the company.
- Provide a brief description of your top management team with detailed résumés in the Appendices as appropriate.
- If you are incorporated, provide highlighted profiles of board members as well.

SAMPLE TEXT

Management

NyTec was quick to recognize that success in the 21st century must be a balance between mainstream business solutions and a competitive power base that rests with flexible and innovative management. The company's five key executives, with a combined 134 years of experience, are highly regarded leaders in their respective fields. Key positions are described below. Highlighted vitas follow with detailed résumés provided in the Appendices, Appendix xx.

The lead paragraph lets readers know something about your company's management strength. Follow this with two or three sentences highlighting key positions and something about each executive's background. Put detailed résumés in the Appendices. Use the same format for all résumés, keeping each to one page or less. Worksheet 29: The Management Team, in the back of the book, is convenient for developing the text for this section. Incidentally, these team members don't have to be employees. It is becoming increasingly popular to outsource executive talent, as discussed under the Advisory Board heading that follows.

If your business plan must double as a fund-seeking proposal, a description of a strong management team is critical, especially in a start-up situation. Both venture capitalists and bankers look favorably on companies that bring industry leaders on board. Such leaders have developed a circle of business friends, can network easily to get to the right sources, and are experienced within their industry — all factors that support the success of your venture.

2. Advisory Board

Writer's Checklist

- First paragraph provides a summary, such as, how many professionals are on your advisory board.
- List all key professionals who advise your company.
- Describe the qualifications of each board member in one sentence followed by a second sentence explaining how each advisor serves the company.

SAMPLE TEXT

Advisory Board

NyTec's management team is enhanced by a highly qualified and accomplished advisory board who specialize in the software and packaging industries. Each of the following six professionals has a minimum of 10 years of experience in their respective fields.

J.L. Smith, CPA, a senior partner in Smith, Collins and Weaver, has held prominent board positions in the software industry for 15 years. Mr. Smith advises the company on all cost accounting matters, current payroll taxes, and regulations.

Advisors offer additional weight in managing a company. Usually the advisory team is a diverse group of consultants: an accountant, industry or product specialists, and design engineers. Others include: information systems and marketing specialists, sales, advertising and public relations professionals, as well as Internet and telecommunication experts, bankers, and insurance agents. There is also a list of attorneys who specialize in business related law, such as corporate and general business, international, trademarks and patents, real estate, and taxes to name a few. Write a formal letter of invitation to advisory board candidates and request a formal letter of acceptance in return. A letter, although not binding in a legal sense, engenders a sense of responsibility.

In certain instances, these advisors offer a new twist to management consulting by acting as part-time executives as well. Both parties win. Companies can save as much as 40 percent on salaries while achieving the same level of performance excellence. The executive, on the other hand, can earn three to four times as much income over conventional employment as an independent contractor, as shown in Figure 5.1. An example for completing Worksheet 30: Advisory Board, is provided together with a corresponding blank in the back of the book.

FIGURE 5.1

Full-time salary	$80,000
Benefits	40,000
Annual total	**$120,000**
Part-time executive/consultant	
$500/day x 3-day week x 48-week/year	72,000
Annual savings to company	**$48,000**
Executive/consultants	
average scale per day	**$500 – $1,500**

WORKSHEET 30: Advisory Board

Name	Describe Association (Describe in three sentences or less)
J.L. Smith, CPA, Senior Partner	J.L. Smith, CPA, a senior partner in Smith, Collins and Weaver, has held prominent board positions in the software industry for 15 years. Mr. Smith advises the company on all cost accounting matters, current payroll laws and regulations.

The same description you develop on the worksheet can be repeated in your business plan in the same way that it is in the sample text. Worksheet 30, in the back of the book, follows the same format as Worksheet 29.

3. Strategic Alliances

Writer's Checklist

- If applicable, identify strategic partners.
- Describe the role, responsibility, added value and duration of agreement for each partner.

- Identify percentage of ownership and/or profit sharing arrangements.
- Identify a key contact person for each.
- Provide pertinent background information for each strategic partner in the Appendices as applicable.

SAMPLE TEXT

Strategic Alliances

NyTec formed a strategic alliance with ABC, Ltd. for a xx percent position in the company. ABC, a leader in its field, adds both technology and marketing support to NyTec's long-term plans. In addition to ABC, NyTec has also formed an alliance with Overseas Planners, a major group responsible for successfully launching popular software packages in foreign markets. In this instance, NyTec licenses its products to Overseas for an annual fee as well as a xx percent share in gross profits.

Martin K. Lyle, vice president of operations at ABC is NyTec's contact. Hagen Copland, senior vice president of international marketing at Overseas is the key contact person at that company. Histories on both companies are highlighted in the Appendices, together with profiles of Mr. Lyle and Ms. Copland.

If you have developed strategic alliances and/or other marketing partnerships briefly explain your role and responsibilities to each other, which can easily be described in one-half of a page or less. Keep supporting documents concise and put them in the Appendix. However, a note of caution: don't overload the Appendices with elaborate and lengthy exhibits.

If you don't have any strategic partners, consider cultivating some alliances. Competing has changed gears in the last few years, becoming more complex. There is little time to foster strong business relationships in a fast-paced market. However, developing the right partnerships can circumnavigate these complexities by enabling partner companies to pool resources.

4. Staffing

Writer's Checklist

- Collectively describe your lead personnel and provide the number of employees in one paragraph.
- Identify the number of employees that telecommute.
- Address any transnational teams, whether they are comprised of associates or employees.

SAMPLE TEXT

Staffing

In addition to its executive management team, boards, and strategic alliances, NyTec has 27 employees. There are five key management positions and four supervisors. Fourteen positions are divided among the computer-aided design, systems engineering, customer relations, and marketing departments. There are three support staff and one part-time person. The marketing department and all but one designer telecommute from seven diverse locations including out-of-state with one in Germany and two in Japan. Each employee has a minimum of five years of experience in his or her fields and all have been employed by NyTec for more than two years.

Describe your supervisory personnel and number of employees in one paragraph as shown in the sample text. Since the way we do business is rapidly changing, job descriptions may have to be rewritten to meet these new opportunities, specifically in the technology, graphic design, sales, and marketing departments. Also address any special issues such as transnational teaming with your international offices or associates, alliances, and trading partners.

Transnational teaming actually began in the early days of the Net — minus the label. More recently, the International Consortium for Executive Development Research (ICEDR), a consortium of 31 international companies and 22 prominent business schools, conducted a two-year study on transnational teaming. Recognizing that "transnational teams are at the heart of the globalization process," the study's aim was to understand and address the needs of transcultural management. Since the Internet has given anyone the opportunity to become a one-person international company — transnational teaming will become increasingly important.

As for employees who telecommute, consider this: Aetna Health Plans' office in Richmond, Virginia increased its claims processing productivity by 29 percent and saved $12,000 in its first year when nearly half of its claims processors began working from home — and this was only one office. Andrea Billups reported in a *New York Times* Regional Newspaper, that IBM not only saved 20,000 jobs, but cut $45 million in real estate costs over two years when employees were allowed to telecommute. By 2001, over 30 million workers will telecommute, according to a survey by the Gartner Group, a computer industry analyst firm.

Telecommuters are not practical for every company, though. Many types of businesses function better in conventional environments where face-to-face contact stimulates creativity as well as productivity. But if virtual offices filled with telecommuters are part of your strategy, company unification is easily maintained using office pods, an Intranet, and Extranet without sacrificing cost-cutting measures.

Office pods, which are small collapsible offices, can be locked up after use and rolled away. Fully equipped, they are ideal for accommodating anyone who needs workspace now and then, such as, your portable executives, employees who visit from time to time, or frequent business guests. The obvious result is saving overhead costs for unused offices and related expenses. At a mean value of $2 a square foot, wasted footage for just one 10 x 12 foot office costs $2,880 a year.

Workflow should also include document handling. Several recent studies compiled by Coopers & Lybrand and published in *PC* Magazine detailed different costs for document handling. In the U.S. alone, we create, disseminate, file, retrieve, reference, and read over four trillion paper documents a year. Even with the means of electronic communication and the hope of a paperless office, this rate is growing by 22 percent each year! Printed materials that become obsolete before they are ever used cost businesses over $5 billion annually, see Figure 5.2. Each business document is copied an average of 19 times accounting for over 81 billion sheets of paper each month; and for every 10 printed pages, only one is ever consulted. Sole proprietors and small companies take note. Hidden lost dollars hurt even more. How much can you afford to lose in these hidden activities?

FIGURE 5.2

Activity	Estimated Cost	Time Spent
Filing or retrieving documents	$28 in labor each time	
Recreating a lost document	$350 in labor per document	
Reading information		5 to 15% per document
Looking for documents		50% per document
Percent of documents lost		7.5% of all documents
Percent of document misfiled		3% of all documents

5. Organization Structure

Writer's Checklist

- Demonstrate the flexibility of new management styles for meeting today's challenges.
- Identify how information is actually circulated throughout the organization.
- Show how teams work together to achieve company goals. Include company outsiders as well as employees, such as, transnational associates, an advertising agency, subcontractors, distributors, and other sales groups.
- Include all functional activities whether they are performed by only one person or many.

SAMPLE TEXT

Organization Structure

NyTec's organization chart is shown in Figure x. Unlike traditional hierarchical structures, NyTec operates exclusively from cell groups. Cells, although singularly focused, overlap in those instances where sharing data and technology can benefit the company. Cell group leaders act as team coaches, and continually interface with one another on the Intranet. This permits information to immediately reach all levels and geographic locations in the organization.

Casey Stengel once said, "The secret of managing is to keep the five guys who hate you away from the guys who are undecided!" All too often, companies make the mistake of operating their organizations with not much more than Stengel's philosophy to guide them while minimizing many of the operational task requirements. Disorganization is the result.

Regardless of size, every business needs to create an organization chart showing the multitude of diverse activities needed to operate the business. Developing the chart helps clarify goals, identify capital requirements, and determine the professional talent needed now and in the future. Worksheet 31: Organization Chart, illustrates one solution. Although a blank companion is provided in the back of the book, you most likely will have to create your own.

If you are not familiar with how these charts are developed, begin by making a list of the tasks that must be accomplished to get your products or services out the front door. Next write down who does what, not necessarily just employees, but associates, advisors and the like. Group similar activities together under an appropriate heading. Decide how information should circulate throughout your organization by evaluating how the information is used. What is the most logical flow of work and information? One of the best ways to do this is to identify the interdependent streams of activities as these activities move through the organization on their way to completion.

Developing a workflow system and sharing it with employees, even in very small enterprises, invites cooperation. An open company structure can be a positive force. Employee enthusiasm increases when they can see how they fit into the overall company structure and why individual job performance is important to the whole. Each person recognizes he or she is an essential contributor. If just one person lets down, it clogs the workflow stream, imposing unnecessary costs and, in severe cases, layoffs. With an understanding of the company's integrated organizational structure, employees willingly take responsibility for their own performance.

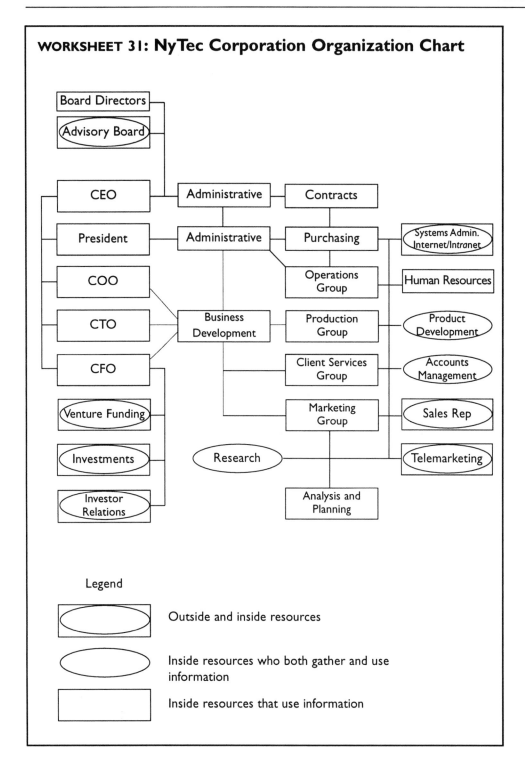

WORKSHEET 31: NyTec Corporation Organization Chart

Board Directors
Advisory Board

CEO — Administrative — Contracts

President — Administrative — Purchasing — Systems Admin. Internet/Intranet

COO — Operations Group — Human Resources

CTO — Business Development — Production Group — Product Development

CFO — Client Services Group — Accounts Management

Venture Funding — Marketing Group — Sales Rep

Investments — Research — Telemarketing

Investor Relations — Analysis and Planning

Legend

⬭ Outside and inside resources

⬭ Inside resources who both gather and use information

▭ Inside resources that use information

Management and Organization Summary

OPTIONAL SAMPLE TEXT

Management and Organization Summary

NyTec's board members and managers are key to its leadership within the industry and the marketplace in general. The seven board members, four advisors, and five executives are supported by six operational cell groups. Each cell is headed by a leader who coaches the group in implementing the company's time-phased objectives.

Information flows vertically and laterally throughout the organization to all 27 employees, executives, advisors, and suppliers via the company's Intranet and Extranet. This allows for immediate reviews, revisions or responses to customers, vendors, buyers, marketing, sales, and personnel.

Answers to the Questions on Page 80

A CSO is a chief sales officer who is responsible for the company's sales force automation (SFA), among other duties. A chief technical officer (CTO) is responsible for all of the company's technology and the chief information officer (CIO) is responsible for all of the data that flows through the company. Portal companies are those that connect users to the Internet, such as Netscape. Commercial websites, with substantial cash flow, are transforming the information systems (IS) executive from that of a front-line technology leader to becoming responsible for the company's bottomline — a major power shift. A CPA's responsibility is well known, whereas, the leadership role of a chief financial officer (CFO) is concerned with identifying, and then successfully acquiring strategic alliances, banking partners, venture funding, and creating the venue for taking a company public.

Writing the Business Plan

SECTION SIX

VI. OPERATIONS
1. Strategy
2. Integrating eCommerce
3. Teams
4. Firewalls

Section Six Objectives

Section Six addresses how the business is managed, its strategy, and how components of the business plan have shaped the company's website. This section includes four different parts and is laid out in the following sequence.

Business Plan Sequence

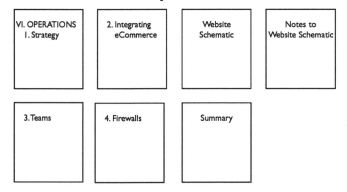

This chapter begins pulling details together that have been developed throughout the planning process. Now is the time to review worksheets completed in earlier sections, especially those relating to the Internet since you will want to include many of these decisions in this chapter.

VI. OPERATIONS

1. Strategy

Writer's Checklist

• Present the details for integrating website activities with existing strategies.
• Briefly outline how the company will be operated.
• Describe the different functions listed on the organization chart.

SAMPLE TEXT

Strategy

NyTec puts customers and employees alike on equal footing for operating a successful company. When translating this philosophy into practical everyday strategies that work, the following has been accomplished:

Internal

• All but eliminated costly employee turnover;
• Increased productivity;
• Created an innovative workforce;
• Decreased sick leave and absenteeism;
• Decreased petty grievances;
• Increased self-esteem; and
• Promoted a friendly and helpful atmosphere.

External

• Repeat customers have increased 35 percent;
• Forty-five percent of first-time customers are from word-of-mouth advertising; and
• Customer satisfaction has increased 100 percent with instant Internet Help Desk.

As noted in NyTec's organization chart, information flows vertically and laterally throughout the organization via the Intranet. Conventional operational strategies, when combined with Internet capabilities, have created new benchmark efficiencies in the following areas:

• **Customer Service:** Custom software is used to identify, track, and interact with individual customers over the telephone or online, thereby improving customer satisfaction and service turnaround time.

The sample text illustrates how to present your company's overall strategy. Notes developed for creating your organization chart can be elaborated on here.

WORKSHEET 32: **Operating Strategies**

Group, Dept., Key Word, or Associates	Strategy	Results
Customer Services	Interactive Immediate/Current Data Restitution	Customer in Control Decreases Frustration Customer Confidence

---

If this is a proposed company, use phrases such as "projected to include," or "will be accomplished."

If needed, add specifics about different departments or groups within the company in a second paragraph. Briefly comment on each, keeping the description to two or three sentences. Use Worksheet 32: Operational Strategy, to further develop key ideas. In addition to company departments, the list might include strategic alliances or advisory board members who are paid to render specific services, a fulfillment house, contract manufacturer — an outsource of any kind.

Successfully implementing any strategy begins and ends with employees who are enthusiastic and want to make a plan work. Operating an eCommerce business can mean giving up an out-of-date hierarchical management system where employees are kept in the dark.

Hierarchical management fits an outdated standard and is costly. In the new organization's structure, employees are informed, from the lowest ranking to the highest. They recognize that their jobs are an important part of the overall whole. Understanding where they fit in and why all but eliminates a perceived loss of control over their jobs. Self-esteem is kept intact. Less absenteeism, employee retention and cooperation results in a productive atmosphere and a prospering company. These, and other findings, were part of two separate job-related health studies.

A research team, headed by Professor Michael Marmot at the University College, London, conducted an eight-year long study of 7,372 men and women. All were civil service employees. Among other things, the team studied the feeling of loss of control as a risk factor in heart attacks. They found that the lack of options is very stressful. As the jobs decreased in stature, the risk of heart attack increased to a staggering 76.6 percent for the lowest-paid from a mean of 9.4 percent for the highest-paid employees.

Another employee-related study conducted by the Meta Group *www.metagroup.com* found company Intranets averaged a 38 percent return on investment, but the organization's culture can affect that return; either decreasing or increasing it.

As part of the new standard, team management now includes the concept of bosses as coaches. Coaches, whether staff members or outside consultants, have the ability to accelerate an employee's learning process and help the individual build self-confidence in both professional and personal arenas. David Lichty, a success coach, put it this way: "Personal coaching is a new answer to a time-tested human learning model. In the past, we learned our trade in an apprenticeship with an expert in the field. In today's fast-paced world, the personal success coach fills this need. There are coaches who specialize in all areas of business available to help you succeed."

Currently, there are 19 coach training institutes in the United States. Most require one year of class work. Corporations around the world are rapidly becoming fans of coaching when they see the impact on their bottom line. Expensive? No, even the smallest business can afford an outside coach. Typically, coaches require a minimum 6-month commitment for a 30-minute coaching session each week. Monthly fees start between $200 or $300. Well-known coaches may cost more. Coaching is provided over the telephone, via email or on-site.

2. Integrating eCommerce

Writer's Checklist

• Present your website.
• Describe each element of the site in a schematic.
• Follow the schematic with "Notes to Figure."

SAMPLE TEXT

Integrating eCommerce

Our internal and external website, illustrated in Figure xx, draws together the varied Internet capabilities described throughout this plan. Those having access to our Extranet and Intranet are given a tracking code together with individual pin numbers. A description for each application is discussed in the Notes following NyTec's website, Figure xx.

This section provides a visual road map of your website, along with a brief description. Worksheet 33: Website Design, is a simple schematic illustrating one way to create website design elements. Follow the design with a "Notes" page to clarify the website graphic. A blank worksheet is provided in the back of the book. If you already have a website homepage, provide a printout; but instead of printing out the whole page, copy it directly from the computer screen.

An easy way to do this is to hold down the "Alt" key on your computer keyboard while simultaneously hitting "Print Scrn" — the key following "F-12" on the top row

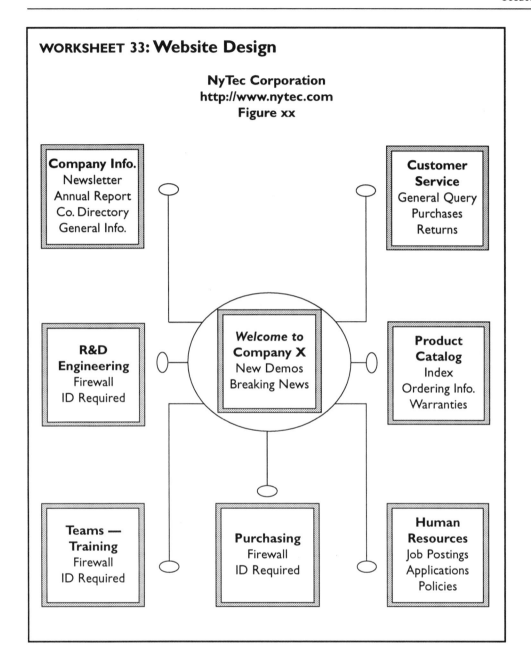

WORKSHEET 33: Website Design

NyTec Corporation
http://www.nytec.com
Figure xx

of keys. This will copy the image as it appears on the Web, tool bars and all. In order to duplicate the image, put your cursor on the page in the business plan where you want the graphic. Hold down the "Ctrl" key while hitting the letter "v" on the keyboard. This will transfer the image to your page. The image may be sized by double clicking it with your mouse. Size as you would any graphic.

Figure 6.1, page 94, shows a typical team needed to create and maintain a website according to a survey by Forrester Research. These professionals might be in-house personnel, subcontractors, or employees of a website development company. The list does not include an online media producer who acts as the coordinator and liaison between management, marketing, and technology. If you are a company of one, you'll wear many hats, so keep the site design simple.

FIGURE 6.1

Job Title	Description	Percent of Contribution
Content Creators	Create webpages and graphics, translate file formats, create animation	55%
Programmers	Write applets, connect sites to databases	30%
Webmaster	Manage content, check links	10%
Marketers	Define direction, evaluate site traffic	5%

SAMPLE TEXT

Notes to Website Design, Figure xx

NyTec Homepage: With one click of the mouse, users have an option from the homepage to link directly to one of the seven website areas.

Company Information: As anticipated, company mailings have steadily declined by xx percent per month since the Internet version has been available. This represents a cost savings in time, printing, materials, storage, postage, and related expenses of $xx. Revisions are constant on the company's website, allowing for a current and accurate delivery system of information to customers. Over time, most of the company's information will be delivered over the Internet.

R&D Engineering: Designated personnel and subcontractors can access certain areas of the website using individual pin codes. This allows teammates to contribute to their respective projects in real-time, without the downtime associated with conventional meetings. Exploratory projects are housed in separate computers and only accessible to members of the engineering department.

Teams — Training: Each team has its own access code to specific webspace on the Intranet. Although this space is secured, teams post updates to the company's bulletin board each Friday. Executive management, and in some instances advisors, can access any area of the website. Training is conducted company-wide via the IntraWeb using the latest audio and video technology. The entire area is protected by a firewall from outside entrance.

Purchasing: Purchasing constantly updates price lists and manages vendors from its online space, also from behind a firewall. Orders can be placed with vendors who have their own Internet presence.

Customer Service: In addition to public inquiry, purchases, and returns, customer service is invisibly linked to the marketing department. This has provided the sales force with information exactly when needed during the sales cycle. As a result, sales turnaround time from introduction to closing has improved 200 percent, growing sales projections beyond expectations. Overall, costs have been reduced by 65 percent in this one area alone.

Product Catalog: Forty percent of NyTec's product line produces 80 percent of its sales. Therefore, the company's entire product line is not graphically displayed on the Web. Popular, sales-producing products are displayed using the latest 3-D Web graphics with animation while the rest of the line is listed by product number only. Once a design is approved by the client, an order form can be accessed from every page or the user may choose to click an icon resembling a shopping cart, which automatically completes the purchase order form. After orders have been shipped, the customer receives an automated warranty template which can be filled out online and returned. The customer database is also designed to reach and inform customers one-to-one, even greet them by name when they return to view NyTec's innovative package designs.

Human Resources: Job openings are posted, together with applications. Selected portions of the company's Policies and Procedures Manual are published on the Web and available to the world at large. This has strengthened the company's Equal Opportunity Employer (EOE) position and met other legal requirements. It also has reduced the time needed for finding and interviewing applicants. Employee records are maintained offline.

Six Ways to Enhance Your Website

There are many ways to enhance your website. Six of the most important ones include the following:

WebPage Size: The main text and graphics of most pages should be about 4 inches high by 5 inches wide when printed out. This doesn't include the copyright notices and contact numbers usually found at the bottom of Webpages in very small print. Users are prone to leave sites if they have to scroll down through a generous amount of text, graphics and advertising, especially on the home page.

WebPage Links: Links within a site should quickly get users where they want to go, not lead to detours or out of the site altogether.

Ego Websites: Many sites scream with self-serving information and don't immediately show users the benefits of reviewing the site's content. Put customer benefits and services first when you are designing your site. Other messages, such as media releases or honors won by the company should not overpower your website.

Simplify: Keep your website simple. Make using it fun, fast, and easy. Consider the golden rule of print advertising as a guideline: you only have a few seconds to catch a reader's attention and sell an idea.

Contact Numbers: Put contact numbers on the bottom of every page in a very small point font. Make it easy, easy, easy for customers to reach you.

Website Sales Tools: Technology is making it possible to manage most anything imaginable right from your site. Select an Internet Service Provider or Web hosting service that offers a wide selection of sales tools if you do not have your own Web department.

Doing business over the Net involves credit card processing, so you'll also need a merchant's account, if you don't already have one. Contact and then compare costs among banks for obtaining and maintaining a merchant's account. Fees vary, so it is recommended you shop around. For your convenience, a blank Merchant's Account (Worksheet 34) is provided in the back of the book for making notes.

Listing Your Site with Search Engines

There are over 800 search engines on the Internet. When you post your website, chances are your ISP will list your company in five or six of the major ones. If you want to be listed with others, you can do it yourself with the right kind of software, such as automated Web page submission software which is available from Kestern Communications Group, *www.submissions.com* or check out *c/net.com www.search.com*.

The following companies will register your site with a multitude of search engines:

www.submit-it.com   *www.submitnow.com*
www.gethits.com   *www.WebPromote.com*
www.register-it.com   *www.websitepromote.com*

SubmitNow! Offers a tutorial for registering sites as well as Search Engine Design Tips from Search Engine Watch. To optimize your listing with the search engines, use TITLE tags, META tags and use a list of key words. The following suggestion was made available from NetScape Communications.

- *Use the TITLE tag.* The text within this tag appears in the title bar of the browser and is the name of the page when it is bookmarked. Many search engines and directories look at this line of text, so make sure that it makes sense and includes a keyword or two.
- *Use META tags.* Many search engines and web guides identify META tags and use the information contained in them to identify the web page and its contents and purpose. There are also services that help you create optimal META tags, such as WebPromote's META Tag Builder and Search Engine Watch's page on How to Use Meta Tags.
- *Use keywords.* Make a list of keywords that relate to your site — think of how other people might try to find you. Keywords can be used when registering your site or with META tags, as outlined above.

3. Teams

Writer's Checklist

- Briefly describe the technology teams use.
- Describe how its used.
- Identify the users by groups as applicable.
- Briefly outline frequency of using the Intranet Activity Planner.

SAMPLE TEXT

Teams

NyTec uses audio and video Intranet teleconferencing to keep teams updated daily. Developed by Cornell University, CU-SeeMe™ is an user-friendly software commercially marketed under several brand names. It allows users from different geographic locations to see and speak with each other over the Internet. The camera, about half the size of a golf ball, currently mounts on top of a computer.

Since the technology is reasonably priced, approximately $200 per unit for color capture and transmission, NyTec provides each employee, all board members and advisors, suppliers, and subcontractors with the product. This has enabled the company to decrease many of its costs associated with training, information sharing, telecommunications, travel, and downtime.

Although a layer of responsibility for training program development has been added together with respective costs, overall efficiency and productivity have increased by 50 percent for both onsite and personnel who telecommute. Growth, with a greater profit spread, has followed.

Coaches meet weekly with their teams and each other. Purchasing interfaces with suppliers as needed. Human resources works closely with new hires and subcontractors while management meets monthly with its advisors. Ongoing training is conducted weekly. Issues that otherwise might not be addressed for some time are brought to the forefront almost immediately giving NyTec an outstanding competitive edge.

One of the most remarkable aspects of the Web is the ability to interactively audibly/visually slice across time and space instantly. CU-SeeMe™ and live streaming media technology have opened a floodgate of teleconferencing possibilities. Although these applications have far-reaching potential, two of the most practical uses are for team projects and training. Traditional training costs can represent as much as 5 percent of payroll. Now, these costs can be drastically reduced. There are companies that specialize in streaming media services. Ask your ISP for a reference.

Assuming your plan will include website teleconferencing capabilities, briefly describe the technology, how it will be used, and by whom. An Intranet Activity Planner (Worksheet 35) follows with a corresponding blank in the back of the book. However, it isn't necessary to include this sheet in your business plan.

4. Firewalls

Writer's Checklist

- Describe your firewall capability — cautiously.
- Demonstrate your firewall strength without giving up confidentiality.

SAMPLE TEXT

Firewalls

NyTec uses both application-based and router-based firewalls to protect sensitive information from both inside and outside intrusion. Extremely sensitive data is stored on separate computers at a undisclosed location. Authorized personnel must meet specified criteria on a continuing basis to reinforce security.

Firewalls are security systems that protect private computer data from unauthorized use. Without firewalls, anyone can access both your public documents and sensitive company data: payroll to accounting records, wholesale prices, supplier information, customer lists, and more. Successful firewalls usually combine both hardware and

WORKSHEET 35: Intranet Activity Planner

12-Month Training and Meeting Plan*

Month	Week 1	Week 2	Week 3	Week 4	Notes
Jan	Coach meet Coach/Team	New hires Orientation M/8–12	Coach meet Coach/Team	Training M/4–5	
Feb	Coach meet Coach/Team	Supplier input	Coach meet Coach/Team	Training T/3–5	
Mar	Coach meet Coach/Team	Supplier input	Coach meet Coach/Team	Training M/4–5	
Apr	Coach meet Coach/Team	Supplier input New hires Orientation M/8–12	Coach meet Coach/Team	Training M/4–5	
May	Coach meet Coach/Team	Supplier input	Coach meet Coach/Team	Training T/2–5	
Jun		Coach meet Coach/Team		Management and Board Training	Vacations start
Jul		Coach meet Coach/Team	Supplier input	Coach Training	
Aug		Coach meet Coach/Team		New hires Orientation M/8–12	
Sep	Coach meet Coach/Team	Supplier input	Coach meet Coach/Team		
Oct	Coach meet Coach/Team	Supplier input	Coach meet Coach/Team		
Nov	Coach meet Coach/Team		Coach meet Coach/Team		
Dec		Coach meet Coach/Team			Holiday slack

* All meetings are from 8–9 A.M. unless otherwise noted. Changes, additions, and training subjects will be announced no less than one week in advance. Address questions to: intra-webmaster@nytec.com.

software to protect data not only from all outside traffic, but user-segments within a company. A firewall should allow only authorized traffic to pass and provide the *only* path between all user networks.

There are two types of firewalls: router-based and application-based. Routers are less expensive, but do not offer the advantages application-based firewalls can. Both are effective, yet neither can protect against sophisticated hackers, viruses, non-network file exports, and the damage done by employees who inadvertently send data to unauthorized persons. The complexity of setting up a firewall varies considerably and can cost as much as $100,000 or more. Do-it-yourself technology is improving daily; however, expert installation is recommended.

The amount of money you budget for Internet security depends upon how much security is worth to you. To find out, start by measuring the cost of installing Internet, Intranet, Extranet, and other computer-related firewall security against an estimated loss, for proprietary information. Worksheet 36: Firewalls, is provided in the Worksheets section in the back of the book. List your risks under the risk assessment column. This most usually includes sensitive marketing data, financial information, or even your business plan. What would it cost you to replace these and what would you be risking in lost opportunities if the data fell into the wrong hands? After determining these risks, it will become obvious what you need to protect, and what software and hardware you need.

Then, after the firewall(s) is in place, contact the Security Assistance Company at *www.icsa.net*. This organization offers a wealth of information as well as a security certification program that tests the hackability of a website. Approved sites will display a SAC certification logo.

Security issues can become even a greater challenge than installing firewalls, especially for conservative law firms with highly sensitive data like Price, Postel & Parma *www.west.net/~ppp*. When a significant number of outside requests for its email address began to mount, this 148-year-old law firm approached Internet security with its own idea of a firewall.

While the firm was already utilizing several proprietary online data and support services, the Internet represented a public architecture — potentially a direct line to sensitive data on hard drives. Each step into the world of eCommerce had to respect organizational philosophy that "change should be consensual and incremental, rather than revolutionary." Key to the project's success meant zero Internet abuse, a budget to match, security, and an underlying respect that some of the attorneys didn't even use a computer. Equally important, one person needed to facilitate this technology expansion.

Under the guidance of techno-attorney Ken Pontifex a simple road to the future has been built one brick at a time. The company began by using an existing, stand-alone old 486 PC, which had formerly hosted the firm's UNIX-based accounting and timekeeping system. It would be the only computer dedicated to Internet use and stand in a high traffic area, unobtrusive yet quite visible. This was a perfect solution for blunting criticism and winning initial acceptance.

The cost, too, was right. "It is easier to build consensus for a new technology if it barely makes a ripple in the firm's technology budget," Pontifex points out. "By relying on dialup access to a remote ISP host in the beginning, security concerns were reduced to a minimum while avoiding the significant expense of building and maintaining a firewall," he adds. In addition, the mailroom staff began routing incoming email, a routine almost unnoticed by the firm's 50 partners and employees.

Although email was the firm's major reason for opening its doors to the Internet, Pontifex knew the Web offered a wealth of research and other data that could benefit the company as a whole. Mindful not to force the issue, he began by creating an Intranet of useful links to legal information which he dubbed *Internet Law Links*.

It soon became obvious that limiting *Internet Law Links* to internal use only limited its potential for enhancing the firm's image and reputation. The easy-to-use instructional Web pages were ultimately added to the website where they are maintained and updated by lawyers rather than technocrats or graphic artists. "Unlike most legal directories, we list only a manageable number of quality websites, " Pontifex explains.

Even though, this conservative law firm expects the Internet to supply an increasingly large share of the communication, data resources and marketing tools it uses for the remainder of its second century, Price, Postel & Parma has no intention of shedding its low-key style. The firm, like many conservative companies, feels it is important to incorporate the latest technologies into its business approach, but not to the exclusion of highly individualized and personal service. As the firm's founder pointed out in 1880, "Great reforms progress slowly." If your firm is conservative yet would like an Internet presence, Pontifex has this advice:

- Don't force email onto every desktop.
- Keep security concerns to a minimum by using a remote dialup Internet service.
- Train several key people to assist new users.
- The Web is "thick with electronic brochures." Stand apart from others in your industry by offering something of value on your site.

By the turn of 2000, Price, Postel & Parma had advanced to a server network with internal and external email. "Things we do at this point provide some current benefits and, importantly for a technology-trailing industry like law, help us to gain knowledge and skills for the future where the pay-off will be greater," observes Pontifex.

OPTIONAL SAMPLE TEXT

Operations Summary

Conventional operational strategies, when combined with Internet capabilities, have created new benchmark efficiencies throughout NyTec. Attributed to the company's website, customer retention and acquisition, sales have outpaced projections while employee productivity has increased considerably.

Housing both internal and external operations, the website is easy to use yet secured behind transparent firewall protection. Outside users have instant access to all public information, job openings, catalogs, ordering, and customer services. Internally, executives, management, coaches, teams, and business associates meet and/or train regularly in virtual real-time using the latest Internet technology for visual, audio and text delivery.

In capsule, by digitally integrating its business to include eCommerce, NyTec has become highly competitive, improved its cash flow, cut costs by a mean of xx percent, while doubling sales within the last six months.

Writing the Business Plan

SECTION SEVEN

VII. BUSINESS LOCATION AND EQUIPMENT
1. Site and Facility Description
2. Suitability to the Business
3. Contractual Agreements
4. Equipment Description

Section Seven Objectives

Section seven discusses the company's location, its facilities, equipment, and why these are suitable to the business. This section includes four different parts and is laid out in the following sequence.

Business Plan Sequence

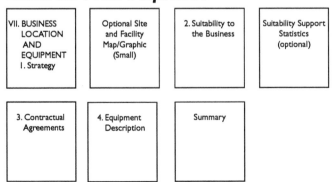

The amount of detail provided in this section depends upon the type of company, its size, and labor requirements. For certain businesses, such as a small service business with a home office, all four sections in this chapter can be combined into one or two paragraphs, whereas, a retailer, distributor, or manufacturing company all with eCommerce on the front burner, will need to address each section in more detail. If you are developing a virtual company and will sell exclusively over the Internet, treat subcontractors the same way you would if they were company departments. Should your plan be doubling as a funding proposal for company expansion, this section is important since investors and/or bankers would want to know how the funds will be spent.

VII. BUSINESS LOCATION AND EQUIPMENT
1. Site and Facility Description

Writer's Checklist

- Briefly describe where the business is headquartered.
- Reference other locations, if applicable, as well as virtual offices.
- If applicable, show the site location on a map.
- If applicable, show the floor plan indicating where equipment is located.

SAMPLE TEXT

Site and Facility Description

NyTec leases a 4,200 square foot office in the Old Town Bank building in addition to a 15,700 square foot facility on Littleton Road. All packaging design activities are conducted in its offices, with printing, manufacturing, warehousing, and shipping maintained in the Littleton facility. A floor plan for the manufacturing facility is provided in the Appendices, Appendix xx.

This is an easy section to write and usually can be done in one paragraph similar to the sample text. Your company's address appears on the inside cover page of the plan making it unnecessary to repeat the address here. If there are several locations, it is sufficient to say "...located in five major shopping malls," or "...15 affiliate offices throughout the country."

If, on the other hand, you are seeking venture capital or a loan for the purpose of purchasing new equipment, expanding your facility or buying real estate, this section of the plan is important. Investors want to know how the money will be used. At times, they will request that a business plan accompany an application for a commercial real estate loan. This may require other bulky documents, such as lengthy escrow papers, leases, or building blueprints in your package. Don't try to bind everything together. Reference the documents in the plan by an Addendum number, such as Addendum A, providing the necessary papers under separate cover. Worksheet 37: Business Location, is the only worksheet for this chapter.

2. *Suitability to the Business*

Writer's Checklist

- Support a location rationale/objective. For example, a high tech firm would need to be near a skilled workforce.
- Justify the location with applicable data, such as, labor statistics for the surrounding area, zoning laws or shipping access.

SAMPLE TEXT

Suitability to the Business

The Old Town Bank building is especially suited to NyTec's needs due to recently installed fiber optic telephone lines for high-speed transmissions, improved parking facilities, overall building security, and the proximity to major thoroughfares. The location is convenient for clients and employees alike, including the company's contributing designers, who telecommute from three virtual offices. The Littleton Road facility is within one block of two major freeways and a large, suitable workforce.

In one paragraph, or two at the most, justify the location's suitability and, where applicable, reference other findings. Add any applicable data, such as labor statistics or zoning laws. If data is lengthy, reference it in the Appendices and/or for small amounts of data use a pie chart. If in doubt, opt on the side of logic. A weighty budget for overly posh offices for a start-up venture may be difficult to explain to investors regardless of how suited it is to the business.

Everything in a plan must have a rationale and support conclusions from other chapters. A location and its suitability to the business are no exception. A rationale for one company may be there is limited competition within a five-mile radius. Another company might need a building that is already equipped for a medical practice; a trucking company needs to be headquartered close to a freeway; a large labor force within 15 minutes driving time is important to one company; or it might be moving to a smaller facility cuts overhead since 35 percent of the employees telecommute. Disaster can also invite relocation.

It was January 17, 1994. Night was giving way to early morning hours when the Northridge earthquake violently awakened Southern California. To many, it signaled both an end and a beginning; for the employees of MetaCreations *www.metacreations.com* it was to introduce a completely new way of life. Their Santa Monica office building was damaged and unsafe, setting into motion a search for new space.

Following his convictions for "an exciting and dynamic work environment," the company's CEO began looking outside of the Los Angeles area. In time, he found a building set on a cliff overlooking the Pacific Ocean in Carpinteria, California — just a heartbeat from Santa Barbara. This prized location meant a higher standard of living for everyone, but undertaking the move presented any number of obstacles.

Moving a single office is difficult enough, let alone a facility with 120 employees at that time. It is a balancing act to "keep everyone informed, up to date and excited about their new home while negotiating with movers and a complex telephone system" according to Todd Buranen, Administrative and Facility Manger, who coordinated the event. Keep in mind too, employees were also moving their households. This meant bending work schedules to accommodate personal needs, finding answers to their important questions, and meeting deadlines as the move neared.

The CEO at that time personally met with each employee, assuring each of his or her role with MetaCreations and answering questions about the move. To further ease the stress Buranen, contacted local Realtors and invited them to make a presentation to employees about their new community. Several weekends were also spent in and around Carpinteria gathering information about the area, its culture, local events and buying newspapers for employees to read. Rental agencies were contacted and listings posted. "The more informed our employees were with their new home, the more at ease they were with the situation," Buranen relates. In the end, 95 percent of MetaCreations employees moved with the company.

The move itself involved many details — for instance, postal permits, signage, phone services, and safe transport of electronic equipment. Surprisingly, the Internet proved to be an invaluable tool for accessing more information on local companies and phone switching equipment than Buranen was able to gather from various sales people.

Timing was very important. All details were to be in place two weeks prior to the move so the company could spend the final days concentrating on the move itself and the installation of its new phone switching system. Over Labor Day, the company closed on Friday afternoon and opened for business on Tuesday morning. Friday was used for packing. The movers picked up and delivered on Saturday and Sunday. Monday, employees installed fax machines, printers, and copiers, beginning the unpacking process.

With the onset of T-1 and ISDN telephone lines, the Internet, voice mail, advanced telecommunication technologies, and the complex telephone units themselves, few are prepared for the challenge of installing a leading edge phone system. Although Buranen rose to the challenge, he readily admits he would not want to go through it again. "There were complications with the new installation. Their first week in the new facility involved numerous and exhausting problems with the phone system."

When asked what he would recommend to other companies undertaking a move, Buranen quickly produced the following checklist:

- Visit the area where you are planning to relocate.
- Find out as much as possible about the community, its schools, special events, housing cost of living — everything that affects the quality of life of your employees.

- Make a checklist with deadlines for all operational aspects.
- Identify perks for the employees at the new site. This can even be a new soda machine or snack machine. Get employees excited about their new location and community. Make them feel a part of the move by keeping them happy and informed.
- Phone installations are complex. Allow twice as long for this as you may have in the past.
- Select the moving company very carefully and get references.

Benefits? The company is extremely pleased with the improved quality of life it has created for employees and their families. The location of its facility is peaceful with ocean views and beautiful sunsets. Smog and freeway parking lots are foreign to Carpinteria residents. It is a slower pace, more relaxed and in tune with the creative atmosphere of the company.

3. Contractual Agreements

Writer's Checklist

- Briefly describe any agreements, most usually leases, that relate to the site or facility.
- As needed, provide one or two paragraphs highlighting contractual agreements in the Appendices or a separate Addendum.

SAMPLE TEXT

Contractual Agreements

The company has a favorable three-year lease for its office space and is currently entering escrow to purchase the 24,000 square-foot building on Littleton Road. NyTec will occupy the same 15,700 square feet previously mentioned, reserve 5,000 square feet for planned expansion during the next 12 months, and will lease the remaining footage to existing tenants. A highlighted summary of the contractual arrangements is provided in Appendix xx. Legal documents are available for review to qualified parties.

Many businesses ignore the need for legal counsel when signing a real estate lease. According to Susan K. Chelsea, a recognized business attorney, the single greatest mistake companies make when entering into a lease is "negotiating a lease term that is too long, thereby, creating a huge liability for the business. Instead, a business should negotiate a shorter lease term with an option to extend it." Chelsea also cautions there are other concerns with leases that can be very costly if not properly negotiated. This includes:

- Estimating the actual costs for tenant improvements.
- Not including a liquidated damages clause if the leased space is not ready to occupy per the lease agreement.
- Negotiating a yearly increase in rent that exceeds the historical market rate.
- Not ascertaining the extent of charges (and past rates) for utilities to be added to the monthly rent payment.

4. Equipment Description

Writer's Checklist

- Briefly describe existing equipment with its related value.
- Briefly describe planned equipment purchases or leasing.
- Provide a detailed list of purchases in the Appendices with the cost and vendor resource; and/or provide the list under separate cover in an Addendum.

SAMPLE TEXT

Equipment Description

NyTec's operations are fully automated. The company owns all computer and printing equipment, which is valued at $xx million. New capital injection will be used to purchase additional computers, printing equipment, upgrade certain hardware, and license new software. A list of these purchases, together with costs and vendor resources is provided in Appendix xx.

If applicable, provide a list of equipment purchases in the Appendices together with costs and vendor resources. Keep the plan text brief, referencing existing equipment in one sentence, if possible.

OPTIONAL SAMPLE TEXT

Business Location and Description Summary

NyTec has 4,200 square feet of office space in the Old Town Bank building with a favorable three-year lease. The company additionally leases 15,700 square feet on Littleton Road for warehousing and printing. Currently, NyTec is in escrow to purchase the 24,000 square foot Littleton facility, reserving an additional 5,000 square feet for its own use and leasing the rest to existing tenants.

The Old Town Bank building is especially suited to the company's needs due to newly installed T-3 lines in the building, parking access, overall building security, and the proximity to major thoroughfares. The location is convenient for clients and employees alike, including Nytec's contributing editors, who telecommute from three virtual offices. The Littleton Road facility is within one block of two major freeways and a large suitable workforce.

The company is fully automated, and owns all computer and publishing equipment, which is valued at $xx million. New capital injection will be used to purchase additional equipment and upgrade certain hardware.

VIII. FINANCIAL PLAN
1. Risk Evaluation
2. Investment Proposal
3. Exit Strategy
4. Break-Even Analysis
5. Financial Projections
   - *Five-Year Projected Profit & Loss:*
   - *Five-Year Projected Cash Flow:*
   - *Five-Year Projected Balance Sheet:*
6. Historical Financials

Section Eight Objectives

Section Eight spells out all of the company's financial conclusions developed from the planning process. It also includes a risk analysis, investment proposal, and exit strategy for venture capital investment. The five sections are laid out in the following sequence. Historical Financials are used for established companies.

Business Plan Sequence

VIII. FINANCIAL PLAN 1. Risk Evaluation	2. Investment Proposal	3. Exit Strategy	4. Break-Even Analysis
5. Financial Projections	6. Historical Financials	Summary	

If your plan is used solely for managing the business, investor or loan information is obviously superfluous. While public companies must meet certain criteria in presenting their financial data, privately held companies may do as they wish. Legal and accounting counsel is recommended though. If you are creating a new company, approximate your actual expenses. Operating budgets and other financial data are usually available through your industry's trade association. Accounting firms specializing in your industry are also a valuable resource.

VIII. FINANCIAL PLAN
1. Risk Evaluation

Writer's Checklist

- Clearly outline any potential losses that might occur.
- Expose any and all information that could have a direct negative impact on the company, causing it to not reach its goals.

SAMPLE TEXT

Risk Evaluation

There is significant risk to the investor given that technology as well as technology delivery systems change rapidly. The Internet as a marketing medium has made history, yet is unproven in the traditional sense. Government regulations could also impact the industry. Worldwide competition will continue to increase, and major corporate conglomerates can afford to duplicate many of NyTec's ideas once they are proven successful. Any one of these events or other unknown circumstances may preclude the company from realizing its sales projections in part or altogether.

This summary does not purport to be complete and is qualified in its entirety by reference to the provisions of an agreement that will exist between an investor and NyTec. A prospective investor should carefully consider the following risk factors and consult with legal and financial advisors prior to considering this investment consisting in part of the following:

Term of the Company: The company is perpetual. However, NyTec may choose to merge with a carefully selected publicly traded entity, a privately held company, or to offer an IPO (initial public offering).

Liability and Indemnity of Principals: Neither the principals nor any of their affiliates will be liable to NyTec or to any of the shareholders for damages attributable to their acts or omissions, except that the principals may be liable for gross negligence or willful misconduct, arising out of or relating to the affairs of the company. This indemnification will be satisfied out of the assets of the company.

Transferability of Interests: An equity investment in the form of privately held stock certificates in NyTec may not be sold, transferred, or assigned without the prior written consent of the majority stock holders. NyTec retains the first right of refusal.

Reports: Shareholders will receive annual audited financial statements for NyTec. Annual tax information necessary for completion of tax returns, and such information concerning the company, may reasonably be requested by a shareholder.

Board of Directors: There are seven seats on the Board. Detailed background profiles of current members are provided in the Appendices of this business plan. Investors, whether one or many of the same group, will receive one Board seat.

Counsel to the Company: A list of counsel to NyTec is provided on the inside front cover of this business plan with contact numbers. Professional background information is provided in the business plan.

On the surface, your company may appear almost risk-free. But look again, as there are many risks associated with doing business. All-night marts and banks are robbed. Companies offer services where employees are put in danger. A competitor can steal ideas. If the competitor has a large financial muscle, you can be knocked out of the game with nothing to show for your effort but a lost opportunity. Even choosing a trademark can be a risky business.

According to attorney Kathleen Corbin (*619-297-9800*), whose practice includes federal trademark registrations, "An error in selecting a trademark or service mark can be very costly in terms of time and money. For instance, you can be forced to stop using the mark because it infringes on someone else's mark or you might choose a mark that cannot be protected from use by your competitors."

The risk evaluation, therefore, is very important for a funding proposal, especially for equity investment. If risks are not pointed out, they have been known to come back and haunt companies when disgruntled investors sue for nondisclosure. The sample text for this section provides some guidelines for the presentation of information, but at this juncture, you are encouraged to seek legal counsel since investor or loan agreements become legal binding documents together with your business plan.

2. *Investment Proposal*

Writer's Checklist

- State who owns the company and to what extent.
- Describe the key financial parameters.
- Indicate how much capital is needed.

- Reiterate the company's description (I. INTRODUCTION, 1. Business Description) since many lenders or investors will review the Financial Proposal first.
- Show how much money the founder has invested.
- State if the company has had other funding, such as initial seed capital, first or second stage equity investors, or loan capital.
- Outline the return on investment that investors may expect.

SAMPLE TEXT

Investment Proposal

The intent of this business plan is to demonstrate to investors the financial merits of investing in NyTec, thereby participating in the returns generated from its product. In support of this plan, NyTec seeks an additional $xxx in equity investment (or loan capital) having already invested $xxx in second stage funding. The new capital will be required immediately and will be used to facilitate the further product and technical development, operations, and marketing described in this business plan. In return for their $xxx contribution, investors will receive xx percent interest in the company and one Board seat.

As a growth-oriented business, NyTec will retain xx percent of its Net Cash Flow in each quarter. These funds will be used for competitive research and new product development specifically addressing the Sure Lock patented software packaging closure. Distributions of earnings to shareholders will commence in the first quarter of 2003. Based on current financial projections and a xx percent share in distributed earnings, investors will receive an attractive xxx percent return on their initial investment over the three-year period. This significant return will be further enhanced by the investor's share ownership in the increasing value of NyTec.

NyTec is the outgrowth of a concept conceived and developed in 1989. Funded with $xx of the founder's money and later with $xx in seed capital, the company incorporated in the state of Texas May 27, 1992, with xxxxxxx authorized shares. There are xxxxxxx shares issued. xx percent of NyTec is owned by its founder and president, D. W. Twit, and xx percent by S.M. Buckman, whose principal place of business is Texas.

Targeting four marketing sectors, NyTec's business is conducted traditionally and virtually over the Internet at <*www.nytec.com*>.

The sample text here is lengthy to show how an investment proposal might be worded. Legal counsel is imperative, especially when negotiating funding contracts. It might seem redundant to reiterate your company's background, but as previously pointed out, 90 percent of the time, lenders or investors will review the Financial Proposal first. Also spell out how much capital is needed and what is the projected ROI (return on investment).

Explain who owns the company, to what extent and the stage of development. Is this a seed start-up, first-stage, second-stage, a mature organization, or something in between? Investors also favor a company whose founder has a lot at stake and whose boards and key management posts are filled with industry experts. This information is eye-catching, encouraging the reader to dig deeper.

3. Exit Strategy

Writer's Checklist

- Describe how founders and investors will dissolve their association if they so choose.
- Identify a date of dissolution.
- If applicable, identify any additional return on investment.

SAMPLE TEXT

Exit Strategy

The intent of this investment is to maximize the shareholders ultimate return by exploiting current and future marketing opportunities. In the event that any or all investors choose to discontinue their financial interest in the company at the end of the three-year period, NyTec will offer to repurchase the investor's shares at a total price equal to xx percent (or the percentage of ownership represented by the shares tendered) of the value of the company as indicated by the Common Stock and Retained Earnings levels in the balance sheet. Based on current financial projections, this stock repurchase will substantially increase the return realized by investors.

In this section, describe how you propose to dissolve your association with investors, if at all. Give dates and add any additional benefits investors will receive.

4. Break-Even Analysis

Writer's Checklist

- Provide a break-even chart.
- Pinpoint the anticipated time frame for breaking even.

Break-Even Analysis

NyTec's break-even analysis for the next 12 months is demonstrated in Figure xx on page xx. As company growth continues, employees are added, and capital equipment debt is reduced, the break-even point will be adjusted accordingly.

FIGURE 8.1: Break-Even Analysis Example

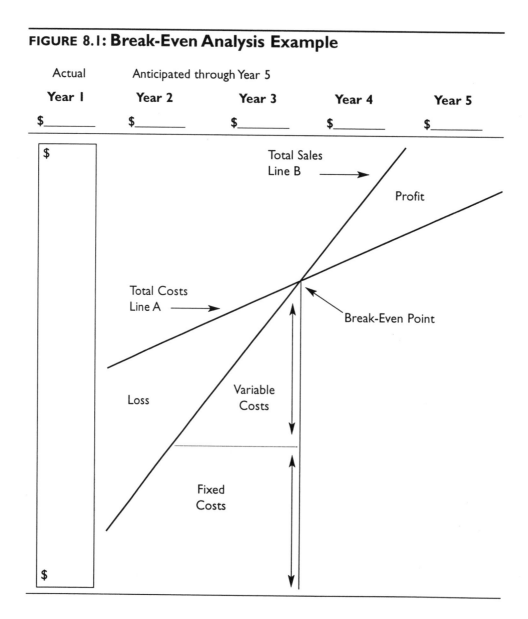

Have your accountant supply a break-even chart with Notes explaining the analysis. If a start-up, it might take several years for the company to break-even! It's optional, but some seed stage or start-up companies project an optimistic and pessimistic outcome, offering another layer of protection from angry investors if things don't work as planned. Figure 8.1 illustrates a break-even chart.

5. *Financial Projections*

Writer's Checklist

- Follow the Five-Year Sales Projection chart.
- Avoid including reams of unimportant financial data.
- Provide the following financial statements:
  - Five-Year Profit & Loss Projections (annual)
  - Five-Year Cash Flow Projections (annual)
  - Five-Year Balance Sheet Projections (annual)
  - 12-Month Profit & Loss (month-to-month in year 1; optional in some plans)
  - 12-Month Cash Flow (month-to-month in year 1; optional in some plans)
- Provide Notes to Financials following the statements or as footnotes on the statements.

SAMPLE TEXT

Financial Projections

NyTec, through its counsel, Smith, Collins and Weaver, has prepared the following financial statements. These statements support marketing projections shown in Figure xx, page xx and other assumptions described throughout this business plan. Notes follow statements.

- Five-Year Profit & Loss Projections (annual)
- Five-Year Cash Flow Projections (annual)
- Five-Year Balance Sheet Projections (annual)

This section mirrors the sales projection chart in Section IV. All of the financial statements are based on future sales covering a three-to-five year period and include the following:

Annual

- Five-Year Profit & Loss Projections
- Five-Year Cash Flow Projections
- Five-Year Balance Sheet Projections

Month-to-Month

- 12-Month Profit & Loss Projections Year 1.
- 12-Month Cash Flow Projections Year 1.

Month-to-month statements based upon Year-One projections are most always required.

The five-year projections used as examples were prepared for *businessplan.com* by the law offices of tax specialist John W. Sunnen, Attorney at Law, L.L.M. (*858-546-4477*), and Judith L. Sigsworth, B.A. and paralegal. The financial analysis, Figures 8.2 through 8.4 is hypothetical and has taken a very simple approach for a start-up business. The company was capitalized with $80,000, which it used to purchase $60,000 of inventory and $20,000 of business equipment in its first year of operation. To simplify the presentation, income tax analysis and accounts for income of self-employment taxes have been deliberately omitted as have entries to report this business on the accrual method of accounting.

With so many outstanding financial software packages it is fairly simple to produce your own statements, including accompanying pie or bar charts that are easy to read. However, operating a company is not about projecting numbers in spreadsheets. You must also have financial-savvy. Using an accounting firm is a plus, and a CFO even better.

Allow leeway for a start-up operation. It takes a good three to four months to open offices, find and hire people, establish work systems, install equipment, and get software and hardware up and working before your doors are opened for business. Then, allow at least another six to twelve months before you have substantial cash flow. "Businesses either have the cash on hand to operate (positive cash) or they must borrow cash (negative cash) in order to operate." In both cases, positive or negative, interest on the money is involved. Allow for this, among other important financial planning decisions.

6. Historical Financials

Writer's Checklist

- Only companies with a financial history are required to provide these statements.
- Include in the plan if essential to funding; otherwise provide this material under separate cover and make it available on request.

SAMPLE TEXT

Historical Financials

Profit and Loss statements for the past three years are provided on the following page beginning in 1998. Note, annual growth has been consistent, even accelerating this past

FIGURE 8.2: Five-Year Profit & Loss

Profit and Loss Statement
New Business
ID #99-XXXXXXX

	Year 1	Year 2	Year 3	Year 4	Year 5
Income:					
Gross Receipts or Sales	$100,000.00	$120,000.00	$140,000.00	$160,000.00	$200,000.00
Returns and Allowances	$2,000.00	$2,000.00	$2,000.00	$2,000.00	$2,000.00
Inventory at Beginning of Period	$—	$24,000.00	$10,800.00	$5,400.00	$7,800.00
Purchases	$60,000.00	$30,000.00	$45,000.00	$60,000.00	$75,000.00
Cost of Items for Personal Use	$—	$—	$—	$—	$—
Cost of Labor	$—	$—	$—	$—	$—
Material and Supplies	$—	$—	$—	$—	$—
Other Costs	$—	$—	$—	$—	$—
Inventory at End of Period	$(24,000.00)	$(10,800.00)	$(5,400.00)	$(7,800.00)	$(10,800.00)
Cost of Goods Sold and/or Operations	$48,000.00	$43,200.00	$50,400.00	$57,600.00	$72,000.00
Gross Profit	$62,000.00	$74,800.00	$87,600.00	$100,400.00	$126,000.00
Other Income	$3,000.00	$3,000.00	$3,000.00	$3,000.00	$3,000.00
Gross Income	$65,000.00	$77,800.00	$90,600.00	$103,400.00	$129,000.00
Expenses					
Advertising	$12,000.00	$15,000.00	$18,000.00	$21,000.00	$24,000.00
Amortization	$—	$—	$—	$—	$—
Bad Debts from Sales/Services	$—	$—	$—	$—	$—
Car & Truck Expense	$800.00	$1,300.00	$1,600.00	$1,800.00	$1,900.00
Cleaning & Maintenance	$1,500.00	$1,500.00	$1,500.00	$1,500.00	$1,500.00
Commissions	$—	$—	$—	$—	$—
Depreciation & Sect. 179	$4,000.00	$4,000.00	$4,000.00	$4,000.00	$4,000.00
Employee Benefits	$3,200.00	$3,200.00	$3,200.00	$4,000.00	$5,000.00
Freight	$—	$—	$—	$—	$—
Insurance	$1,800.00	$1,800.00	$1,800.00	$1,800.00	$1,800.00
Interest (Mortgage)	$—	$—	$—	$—	$—
Interest (Other)	$1,750.00	$1,750.00	$1,750.00	$1,750.00	$1,750.00
Legal & Professional	$2,000.00	$2,000.00	$2,000.00	$2,000.00	$2,000.00
Office Expense	$1,200.00	$1,500.00	$1,800.00	$2,100.00	$2,400.00
Pension/Profit Sharing	$—	$—	$—	$—	$—
Rent (Machinery/Equip)	$1,600.00	$1,600.00	$1,600.00	$1,600.00	$1,600.00
Rent (Other)	$800.00	$800.00	$800.00	$800.00	$800.00
Repairs	$600.00	$600.00	$600.00	$600.00	$600.00
Supplies	$3,200.00	$3,200.00	$3,200.00	$3,200.00	$3,200.00
Taxes	$918.00	$918.00	$918.00	$918.00	$918.00
Travel	$—	$—	$—	$—	$—
Meals/Ent (50%)	$—	$—	$—	$—	$—
Utilities	$3,200.00	$3,200.00	$3,200.00	$3,200.00	$3,200.00
Telephone	$4,500.00	$4,500.00	$4,500.00	$4,500.00	$4,500.00
Wages	$15,000.00	$15,000.00	$18,000.00	$21,000.00	$24,000.00
Total Expenses	$55,068.00	$61,868.00	$68,468.00	$75,768.00	$83,168.00
Net Profit or (Loss)	$9,932.00	$15,932.00	$22,132.00	$27,632.00	$45,832.00

FIGURE 8.3: Five-Year Cash Flow

Cash Flow Analysis
New Business
ID #99-XXXXXXX
Tax Year: Year 1

	Year 1	Year 2	Year 3	Year 4	Year 5
CASH IN					
Cash on Hand 1/1/YR	$ 80,000.00	$ - 49,932.00	$83,064.00	$114,596.00	$143,828.00
Checking Accounts 1/1/YR	$	$	$	$	$
Savings Account 1/1/YR	$	$	$	$	$
Rental Income	$	$	$	$	$
Schedule C Gross Receipts	$ 101,000.00	$121,000.00	$141,000.00	$161,000.00	$201,000.00
Loan Proceeds	$	$	$	$	$
Interest Income	$	$	$	$	$
Dividend Income	$	$	$	$	$
Schedule D, Sales Proceeds	$	$	$	$	$
Alimony	$	$	$	$	$
Cash Distributions from S Corps & Partnerships	$	$	$	$	$
Other:	$	$	$	$	$
Cash In Flow	**$ 181,000.00**	**$170,932.00**	**$224,064.00**	**$275,596.00**	**$344,828.00**
Total	**$ 181,000.00**	**$170,932.00**	**$224,064.00**	**$275,596.00**	**$344,828.00**
CASH OUT					
Cash on Hand 12/31/YR	$ 49,932.00	$ 83,064.00	$114,596.00	$143,828.00	$190,660.00
Checking Accounts 12/31/YR	$	$	$	$	$
Savings Accounts 12/31/YR	$	$	$	$	$
Schedule C Expenses	$ 51,068.00	57,868.00	$64,468.00	$71,768.00	79,168.00
Rental Expenses	$	$	$	$	$
Schedule F Expenses	$	$	$	$	$
Asset/Investment Purchase	$ 80,000.00	$	$45,000.00	$60,000.00	$75,000.00
Auto, Trucks, Boats	$	$	$	$	$
Estimated Tax Payments	$	$	$	$	$
Gifts	$	$	$	$	$
Medical Expenses	$	$	$	$	$
Real Estate Taxes	$	$	$	$	$
DMV Fees	$	$	$	$	$
Mortgage Interest	$	$	$	$	$
Employee Business Expenses	$	$	$	$	$
Tax Preparation Fee	$	$	$	$	$
Loan Payments	$	$	$	$	$
IRA/SEP Contributions	$	$	$	$	$
Other:	$	$	$	$	$
Cash Out Flow	**$ 181,000.00**	**$170,932.00**	**$224,064.00**	**$275,596.00**	**$344,828.00**
Total	**$ 181,000.00**	**$170,932.00**	**$224,064.00**	**$275,596.00**	**$344,828.00**

FIGURE 8.4: Five-Year Balance Sheet

Comparative Balance Sheets
New Business
ID #99-XXXXXXX

	12/31/YR1	12/31/YR2	12/31/YR3	12/31/YR4	12/31/YR5
ASSETS					
Cash	$ 49,932	$ 83,064	$114,596	$143,828	$190,660
Trade notes/Accounts receivable					
less; Bad Debts					
Inventories	$ 24,000	$ 10,800	$ 5,400	$ 7,800	$ 10,800
U.S. Government obligations					
Tax-exempts					
Other current assets					
Mortgage/real estate loans					
Other investments					
Buildings and depreciable assets	$ 20,000	$ 20,000	$ 20,000	$ 20,000	$ 20,000
less: Accum Amort.	$ (4,000)	$ (8,000)	$ (12,000)	$ (16,000)	$ (20,000)
Land					
Intangible assets					
less Accum Amort.					
Total Assets	**$ 89,932**	**$105,864**	**$127,996**	**$155,628**	**$201,460**
LIABILITIES AND EQUITY					
Accounts payable					
Mortgages, notes, bonds ,1 yr					
Other current liabilities					
Loans—other	$ 80,000	$ 80,000	$ 80,000	$ 80,000	$ 80,000
Capital account					
Current period net income (loss)	$ 9,932	$ 25,864	$ 47,996	$ 75,628	$121,460
Total Liabilities and Equity	**$ 89,932**	**$105,864**	**$127,996**	**$155,628**	**$201,460**

year. In light of this history, NyTec does not consider its future projections ambitious, although the annual percentage growth rate is outside the traditional norm.

This section is used for an existing company with a financial history. For a funding proposal, a financial history is a prerequisite and usually makes the difference between being funded or not. Some companies automatically offer these sensitive documents under separate cover. The same is true of personal financial histories and statements. Offer historical financial documents when asked by serious contenders, otherwise use caution when exposing these data.

OPTIONAL SAMPLE TEXT

Financial Plan Summary

NyTec anticipates a growth rate of xx percent in each of the following three years with an acceleration of xx percent in Year Four and xx percent in Year Five, an increase of annual gross sales in Year One from $ xx to $ xx in Year Five. This translates into an attractive xx percent return on initial investment over the next five years based on current financial projections and a xx percent share in distributed earnings.

Funding and Internet Resources

This section of *businessplan.com* is intended as a guide for locating funding resources. However, space would not permit including the thousands of reputable banks, financial institutions, government guarantee programs, and equity investors in this country or worldwide. Networking is a proven way to find a potential match. Those resources listed here are presented as a place to start. Public libraries offer a wealth of reference books and, of course, the Internet itself is a global resource.

The Funding Treasure Hunt: What You Need to Know

Twenty-three years ago Professor Mohammad Yunus founded the Grameen Bank in Bangladesh *www.citechco.net/grameen/index.html* by introducing the concept of helping the poor start micro-businesses. These no-collateral loans let minute enterprises borrow as little as $50. At the time, Yunus' idea went against the grain of traditional banking. Today, it is praised the world over with hundreds of life-changing success stories — stories like Laili Begum's.

Seven years ago Begum was penniless. Desperate, she courageously borrowed $200 from Grameen Bank to start a grocery store in the village of Patia, just outside Dhaka, India. Today her store is flourishing, her loan is repaid and she proudly owns 36 chickens and four cows. Recently, she borrowed another $430 to open a second business.

A highly charged growth company may not measure success by Begum's yardstick, yet would agree it is access to money that opens the door to opportunity. Ironically, many business people stumble around because they fail to see that the key to successfully accessing money is knowing where to look. In this instance, Grameen Bank was in the market to loan Begum $200, and later $430. Supply and demand went hand-in-hand.

Halfway around the world on the central coast of California, Santa Barbara Bank and Trust's (SBBT) International Banking Group *www.sbbt.com* and Senior Loan

Officers are meeting with one of its rapidly growing business customers. Since the majority of community banks do not offer international departments, the customer is fortunate that SBBT is unique in this one aspect. When the meeting is over, the group will have a strategy to position the company for global expansion.

SBBT has become more than a part of the customer's advisory team; this community bank will, in one sense, become a partner to its success. Both will profit from the association because, luckily, the customer knew "where to shop." Like Grameen, SBBT was in the market to provide what its local business customer needed, value added financial services for both traditional and international banking.

Is this type of personal attention unusual for a bank? For some, perhaps, but not for the majority of community banks specializing in niche markets. According to Tom Thomas, president of SBBT, "Knowing the customer is key at the community bank level."

Both Grameen Bank and SBBT serve select markets, taking particular care to create financial products that meet the needs of their respective customer base. The same is true of most, but not all, multinational, regional, and industry-specific banks or other financial institutions.

Where you look for a strong banking relationship, therefore, depends on what you need, the size of your company, and your track record. There has to be a fit in terms of supply and demand. Personalities matter too. Choosing a bank whose marketing policy is to help your company grow is important, since a banking relationship will always be part of your business, even if a loan isn't part of your present financial plan. eCommerce introduces yet another form of banking: exchanging product for payment over the Internet, in addition to online banking.

As an executive vice president of a regional bank said, "Smart business people know when to borrow money and how much." Though varied to meet a bank's criteria, business loan decisions are usually based on the traditional bankers' Five Cs of Credit: Character, Credit, Cash Flow, Capacity, and Collateral.

- **Character:** How have you managed your personal credit obligations? Personal credit information provides a lender with a quick snapshot of a potential borrower.
- **Credit:** What is your business credit history? Have suppliers and others been paid on time?
- **Cash Flow:** As a rule of thumb you must have $1.50 in cash flow for every $1.00 in loan payments. Your debt-to-income ratio should be less than 50 percent. Ask your financial advisor or banker how they compute cash flow or debt-to-income ratios.
- **Capacity:** In a business downturn, what is your second resource for repayment?
- **Collateral:** What assets will be used to secure the loan?

In addition to banks, there are many other financial resources, such as, Small Business Investment Corporations (SBIC), plus dozens of state and federal loan guarantee programs. Some programs help companies buy commercial real estate, export or even start businesses. Many are represented in this section with contact numbers.

If you opt for equity over debt financing, look to venture capitalists, angels and strategic alliances. Venture capitalists and angels are further discussed in the pages that follow. Strategic alliances are somewhat different. They run the gamut from a loosely defined value-added reseller or (VAR) to a clearly defined binding legal partnership. The most common alliances include the following:

- Joint ventures
- Manufacturing pacts
- Licensing deals
- Marketing and distribution arrangements
- Research and development agreements
- Equity investment

Each type of alliance offers specific advantages. All have risks. Some companies utilize a combination of two or more alliance-types depending on the complementary needs of the companies involved. The most risky are equity investments and joint ventures. Marketing and distribution arrangements are the least risky followed by licensing and R&D. Most business libraries offer a selection of books detailing strategic alliances. Seek legal council from firms specializing in this area.

The smaller/larger alliance is typical for obvious reasons. Smaller companies have greater agility in many important operational areas. Critical or time-sensitive decisions can be made with rapid-fire turnaround. Larger companies, on the other hand, offer credibility, market-power, and clout that small companies seldom have time to grow or simply cannot get on their own. Deep pockets don't hurt either.

In taking the first step toward seeking an alliance, determine your objectives. This will identify the type of alliance needed. Then, ask yourself why your company is unique and identify your barriers to growth. Next, develop a list of 25 prospects. Rank each one in terms of congruous goals and proceed from there. It also helps to enlist the services of a professional who specializes in strategic alliances.

Main Street: Where to Look for Money

Along with Web related partnering opportunities, new investment rules in tax reform, the money supply, and changing criteria among venture capitalists funding opportunities are shining favorably on companies, particularly technology and Internet-related enterprises.

Tax reform has enhanced the advantages of Chapter S corporations. For the first time, pension plans and other tax-exempt entities are encouraged to invest in small private businesses based in part on the 1996 Small Business Job Protection Act. Even more favorable, the stockholder limit has been moved from 35 to 75, with the added benefit of counting a tax-exempt entity as one stockholder. There are other promising aspects as well.

Equally good news, is the money supply and the favored status of smaller companies. The financial industry has been on its best behavior since its debacle in the late 1980s and early 1990s. Simultaneously, corporate downsizing and consolidations have decreased the demand for credit. This has resulted in more money to lend, which in the past was reserved for large corporate customers — but many are now gone. Hello-o-o, small business.

Although most venture capitalists want to cash out in four years or less now, they are nonetheless willing to take a lesser equity position in the company than in the past. The dynamics of emerging technologies and successful IPOs, making billions almost overnight has affected how fast investments can pay off and also has left VCs with an overabundance of money.

If an initial public offering (IPO) is in your future, "Don't let IPO phenoms prompt you into rushing your own public offering. First stake your position. Intelligent positioning is the backbone of a successful IPO and continues to support the company after it is public," according to Robert (Bob) Weaver head of the technology group at Deloitte & Touche LLP. Two of the most often overlooked steps include "building a solid management team" and creating the "proper infrastructure."

Weaver points out, "It is not uncommon for new companies to delay hiring their CFO until just before the IPO process. If you do this, you are doomed to play catch up in building your information systems and other infrastructure operations. You also need an experienced sales executive. Without this executive you cannot accurately forecast sales, an inadequacy that can set in motion a potentially devastating chain of events ... even shareholder lawsuits."

As for building a proper infrastructure, Weaver a 30-year international technology guru, offers this advice, "Today's truly great companies use information to gain a competitive advantage. without adequate information systems in place, you will have trouble meeting your periodic reporting requirements. You will also not have the timely operating results data you need to make (informed) management decisions. Also pivotal to your infrastructure are controls and processes, which are needed to ensure your transactions are in line with management's policies and shareholders' best interests."

Not as new but little known, the government has made it possible for small companies to go public without the traditional cost and red tape — enter Small Corporate Offering Registration (SCOR). This program sidesteps the Securities Exchange Commission (SEC). Governed by each state, it enables small businesses to raise up to $1 million a year by selling common stock to the public, including selling it over the Internet. An assortment of fees, from attorney billings to filing costs, though, are roughly $35,000 to $40,000 and there is still some red tape. In addition to SCOR, ACE-Net, offers a venture capital matching service. Funded by the U.S. government, it brings entrepreneurs seeking between $250,000 and $5 million together with private investors. It may be accessed over the Internet.

Venture capital networks and clubs have recently become a popular way for individual investors to find opportunities. The network brings capital-seeking companies together with investors by soliciting business plans. The plans are reviewed and if response is favorable, Executive Summaries are distributed among the members. Interested investors contact companies directly for more details. Most business libraries offer a selection of books about VC resources. The following list is a small representative sample of VC Networks:

- **Accelerate**
  Irvine, CA 714-509-2990
- **The Capital Network**
  Austin, TX 512-305-0826
- **CONNECT®**
  La Jolla, CA 619-534-6114
- **Environmental Capital Network**
  Ann Arbor, MI 734-996-8387
- **Technology Capital Network at M.I.T.**
  Cambridge, MA 617-253-7163
- **Northwest Capital Network**
  Seattle, WA 206-441-3123

Moot Corp® is the grandfather of business plan competitions. To culminate their MBA entrepreneurial studies, students "from the best programs in the world present their business plans to panels of investors." Many past winners in this prestigious program have translated their plans into real world successes. For additional information about sponsorship, participation, or investment opportunities, contact Dr. Gary M. Cadenhead, Director, Moot Corp®, Senior Lecturer in Entrepreneurship, Graduate School of Business, The University of Texas at Austin, *512-471-5289*; *http://uts.cc.utexas.edu/~mootcorp*.

National Association of Women Business Owners, together with Wells Fargo Bank, offers loans from $5,000 to $25,000 to women business owners. The program was funded with $1 billion. Applications may be made by phone at *800-359-3557*, ext. 120.

Newcourt Financial, formerly AT&T Capital Corporation, is one of the world's leading sources of asset-based financing, with a global distribution capability in more than 20 countries. This little-known capital resource serves the corporate, commercial and institutional markets with nearly $30 billion in owned and managed assets. They also make SBA guaranteed loans, *800-713-4984*.

The World Bank, as well as state programs, also guarantee an assortment of programs geared toward the exporter. One of the most valuable guarantee programs from the World Bank provides financial protection for companies doing business in politically volatile areas and is administered by the World Bank's Investment Guarantee Agency (IGA), *202-473-2426*.

The Money Store is a publicly traded company with 185 branches nationwide. Among other types of loans, the company specializes is SBA guaranteed loans, *800-486-8953*.

GE Capital, an international corporation with 110 offices nationwide, provides a wide range of both loan and equity programs. GE Capital's Capital Equity Group, highly reputable though not as well known, offers an unique strategic investor opportunity from $5 million to $50 million for a minority ownership stake. Their interest in helping companies succeed "goes beyond financing" — a plus for bypassing traditional door-knocking and connecting with the right resources, *888-809-8500*.

Edwards Directory of American Factors lists some 200 factoring companies in the U.S. and is available at most libraries or from the publisher for $200 plus shipping. Factoring is a quick way to access cash, but is expensive at 1.5 to 5 percent of the face value of accounts receivable, *800-963-1993*.

Employee Stock Ownership Plans (ESOP) also offers another way to raise money, and is popular with customers. For state chapters and more information contact the ESOP Association *202-293-2971*; the National Center for Employee Ownership at *510-272-9461*; or the Foundation for Enterprise Development *www.fed.org*.

Small Business Investment Companies (SBIC) was formed in 1958 by the U.S. Small Business Administration (SBA). For every dollar invested by a SBIC in a company, the SBA will match the investment up to 300 percent. With this money, the SBIC forms SBA-guaranteed debentures which are sold to investors. SBICs are usually owned by a group of venture capitalists; however, some commercial banks own SBICs as well. Contact your local SBA office (usually listed in the White Pages under the U.S. Government heading) for a list of SBICs.

Special Small Business Investment Companies (SSBIC) is a step-sister to SBIC, though not as well known. Like SBICs, they are privately owned investment firms licensed and regulated by the SBA, but focus on funding socially or economically disadvantaged companies. There are about 120 SSBICs nationally; a directory is available for $30. For more information about SSBICs, contact the National Association of Investment Companies (NAIC) at *202-289-4336*, 111 14th Street, N.W., Suite 700, Washington, DC 20005.

SBA-Guaranteed Loan Programs loan programs include the following: 7(a) Guaranty: the standard loan program; LowDoc: Low Documentation loan program; Capline: lines of credit including builders, contract, seasonal and asset based; 504: see Certified Development Corporation in this section; EWCL: Export working capital loans; M/W Pre-Qual: minority and women's pre-qualification loans. Not all lending institutions manage all types of loans. Inquire first. Other symbols: CLP: SBA certified lender; PLP: SBA CLP lender with preferred status (independent approval authority for 7(a) guaranty loans). SBA loan programs are well-known as most banks across the U.S. participate in them. It isn't generally known, however, that the programs can require considerable time, paperwork, and collateral. Begin early. The Small Business Administration is listed in the white pages under U.S. Government or online at *www.sbaonline.sba.gov.*

Certified Development Corporation (CDC) is a certified lender for the SBA 504 Loan Program which is an owner-user real estate financing program for small business. The SBA defines a small business as a company with less than $6 million net worth and less than $2 million profit after taxes. Most local businesses meet these standards. CDC's work with primary lenders (mostly banks), who provide a 50 percent senior position, with the CDC providing 40 percent in a second position. Funds can be used for land acquisition, building construction, purchasing an existing building, renovation, equipment purchase providing it is part of the property, and interim loan costs. Part of the criteria for qualification includes creating one job within two years for every $35,000 of the SBA 504 portion of the project's financing. Projects can go as high as $2,426,025. This is an excellent program with low fixed interest rates, and reasonable collateral requirements, with 90 percent financing for most projects. In order to obtain 504 financing, a business must have the sponsorship of a CDC. There are 2,000 nationwide. For more information contact the SBA in your area for the CDC nearest you or search *www.sbaonline.sba.gov.*

National Small Business United formed in 1937, has 65,000 members through its chapters and affiliate organizations. The group maintains small business statistics and strives to keep small business owners in touch with legislative and regulatory issues, *202-293-8830.*

The Business Consortium Fund, Inc. was created to help certified minority supplier-members access working capital, *212-243-7360.*

National Federation of Independent Businesses (NFIB), which was founded in 1943, has an audited membership of 600,000 business owners. The organization was created to give small and independent businesses a voice in governmental decision making, *202-554-9000.*

U.S. Chamber of Commerce offers a free 154-page guide to obtaining financing that lists private, federal and state funding resources. Also ask for a catalog of other publications that offers a wealth of information. Contact an accredited local chamber of commerce or the U.S. Chamber at *202-463-5503.*

Telecommunications Reports International, Inc. (TRI) was first published in 1934. TRI is considered the premier publisher of news and information services for the multimedia, communications, and electric utility industries, *202-842-0520.*

Capital Access Programs (CAP): Loans are available in many states. These programs are designed to assist small businesses that may fall outside of most banks' conventional underwriting standards. A maximum loan amount is $2.5 million. Ask your banker or your state's small business development office. Look in the white pages under State Government for the small business development office.

The Small Business Financial Resource Guide provides private and government contact information to financial resources for each state plus several useful chapters on how to obtain financing. Available from Braddock Communications, Inc. Reston, VA. *www.bradcom.com*

Internet and Business Websites: Links to Funding

In addition to listing your own company on a search engine, you most likely have discovered key word searches will rapidly produce a wealth of business websites and information in pursuit of funding. The financial world has become homogeneous, so think globally when searching for money and other business information. Also think specifically, since most VCs have a narrow range of investment interests. It takes time, so give yourself plenty of it to develop a list of prospects, query them using the one-page Business Plan Summary, Appendix B, and then follow up accordingly.

Other Useful Business Websites

Small Business Advancement National Center, housed at the University of Central Arkansas, is an award winning business website full of useful data from industry profiles to international business. *www.sbaer.uca.edu/*.

The Executive Committee Worldwide, Inc. (TEC) is an international organization founded in 1957 and the first of its kind to provide ongoing CEO education and development through confidential forums where members learn from each other. Membership in either of TEC's two CEO programs is by invitation only. TEC's power comes from the knowledge and experiences shared by the members in each group as they set strategies and make major decisions for their individual companies. The group's confidential discussions are moderated by a facilitator who is an experienced business professional, and often a former CEO himself or herself. Most meetings also include experts sharing cutting-edge ideas and information on subjects the group requests. *www.tecceo.com*.

American City Business Journals lets users access 38 regional business journals and sample hundreds of local business stories. A good tool for preparing media releases. *www.amcity.com/.*

Central and Eastern Europe Business Information Center (CEEBIC), U.S. Department of Commerce, is a business facilitation program for U.S. firms interested in expanding into the Central and Eastern European markets. CEEBIC disseminates high-technology information, and its Washington-based trade specialists and staff in 14 countries provides individualized business counseling. CEEBIC's extensive Internet home page and automated fax-on-demand system provides recent economic and commercial information (including cables from U.S. Embassies in the region), trade leads, and contacts. CEEBIC also has a Small Business Support Facility. For a monthly newsletter or other information, contact CEEBIC at *202-482-2645*; *www.mac.doc.gov/eebic/ceebic.html* or send email to: *ceebic@ita.doc.gov.*

Trade Information Center U.S. Department of Commerce: Provides information about all federal export assistance programs, as well as country and regional market information. To receive personal export assistance from a trade specialist Monday through Friday 8:30 A.M. to 5:30 P.M. Eastern time telephone *800-USA-TRADE* or visit the center's website at *tradeinfo.doc.gov.*

VIBES: Virtual International Business and Economic Sources, created and maintained by J. Murrey Atkins Library, University of North Carolina, Charlotte NC 28223, links to over 1,300 free sites containing data on international business plus U.S. business and economic resources. *libweb.uncc.edu/ref-bus/vibehome.htm.*

WebWrite: Writing HTML and Beyond — Manuals and Resources, University of North Carolina at Charlotte. This is one of the best and most comprehensive websites on the Internet for learning how to create, manage, and design sites. The resources are free covering everything from CGI, JAVA, and JavaScript tutorials with cut 'n' paste scripts to Web page and site design instruction including a section on "how to create Image Maps." *libweb.uncc.edu/ref-arts/webwrite/.*

Information Technology Association of America (ITAA): Founded in 1961, the organization offers many outstanding benefits including advocacy programs, management conferences, domestic and international studies, market development, and industry promotion. ITAA also provides extensive opportunities for business development, particularly for smaller firms seeking partnering relationships, equity financing, joint technology development, or marketing arrangements. With over 11,000 direct and affiliate member companies, ITAA is the leading trade association serving the information technology industry with four divisions: the Software Division; Information Technology Services Division; Information Services and Electronic Commerce Division; and the Systems Integration Division. *www.itaa.org.*

Women in Technology International (WITI): Founded in 1989, WITI is a successful and active organization working closely with industry leaders to help women develop core competencies in demand at all levels of technology organizations. Among other benefits to its members, WITI brings women to the attention of organizations and boards looking for strong talent and is dedicated to increasing the number of women in executive roles. Highly recommended for women in technology. *www.witi.org.*

Internet Wire is the first and largest Internet-based press release distribution service. They manage your digital media needs to contact business and technology editors or reporters. Rates are reasonable and the company will handle as little as one release at a time, *800-774-9473. www.gina.com/.*

A Note of Caution

Opening the flood gates to eCommerce, has also opened the door to financial Internet scams (change the "a" to "u" for a more accurate description). On the Internet, it is very easy to circumvent the law, (avoiding mail fraud charges, for example). Among other scams, con artists prey on businesses in need of funding. Operating under the guise of legitimate investment and money brokers, few have the appropriate credentials. They are highly skilled sales people who exploit the weakest link in a company — a need for money.

They know exactly how far to go and how to make the deal sound credible by zeroing in on want satisfaction. A buyer wants something badly and will make a buying decision based on having that want satisfied. Beware of requests for money up front with promises of easy capital acquisition or too many compliments about your business. Once you are hooked, scams waste important problem solving time plus fragile resources.

There are any number of schemes and presentations which sound or look legitimate, including booths at trade shows. The Better Business Bureau (BBB) publishes a guide about the most popular money-broker scams. Ask your local BBB. Report scams to the Federal Trade Commission. The number is listed in the front of your telephone directory White Pages under U.S. government.

What Investors Look for in a Company

There are some obvious, yet overlooked, reasons why investors opt to fund one company over another. For example:

Turn On's

- Experienced management team in field seeking investment
- A concise risk assessment
- A reasonable return on investment (ROI)
- Evidence that there is a market for the product or service
- A manageable product mix
- Proprietary market position, such as a patent, copyrights or trademarks
- Competitive innovation that sustains company growth
- Realistic expectations and financial projections

Turn Off's

- Hype and unrealistic expectations
- Poorly developed ideas and business plan
- Prices not competitive
- Underdeveloped management strategy
- Inexperienced key people
- Excessively rapid growth that is capital-consuming

Incidentally, a ruling by the U.S. Supreme Court in 1998 has made it possible to patent "business methods." By year's end 1999 key patents for protecting well known intellectual property, such as Amazon.com, Priceline.com, and Open Source, were in place. This will forever change the nature of eCommerce on the Web.

It is easier to sidestep the many false starts in your attempt to locate funding when you come from a point of power. Power is nothing more than feeling secure that your company and its capabilities are rock solid. There are any number of ways to combine funding where each strengthens the other and the company overall. For instance, a strategic alliance might not bring money to the table but can produce a strong marketing and distribution channel. Another alliance could add technical clout and equipment. Professionals who have had successes in your field could be offered stock in the company and an executive position when funded. In exchange, they lend their names, know-how and contacts.

Funding becomes relatively easy when investors see that your company is supported by a combination of successful professionals, good ideas, and alliances with established companies. You can also time capital injection to meet predetermined milestones, such as seed capital to pull the idea together and bring it to stage one whereby the company becomes operational, that is, everything in the start-up phase has come full cycle and you are ready for the next step.

During the seed stage, companies work toward setting the company in motion, finding and hiring a complementary blend of talent, setting all the elements in place to produce a quality product at a competitive price, and writing and implementing the first activities of a detailed time-phased marketing plan. The length of time required to successfully work through seed and start-up phases varies. Obviously, not all business blueprints are alike.

During stage one, many companies are now planning to go public. As noted earlier, once underway you may want to raise additional capital by taking advantage of the SCOR program. In other situations, a traditional IPO would be better. These activities have a lot of investor appeal as well.

Now that chunks of the company have settled in someone else's pocket, what's left for the founder? Usually a much smaller percentage than planned, something that isn't too appealing to many entrepreneurs. But taking a company from here to there is more than talent, products, and money. It is also a mind-set. A top-floor mind-set gets bigger results. These visionaries understand that a small percentage of a tight, viable package is worth much more in a shorter period of time than a large percentage of loosely woven probabilities and limited capital.

On a final note, a good chief financial officer is indispensable since good money management is key to the company's financial health. Many entrepreneurs mistakenly assign this task to a CPA firm. CPA firms are about tax laws and accounting, not necessarily managing the company's capital needs or reserves, although some do that too. Success is the outgrowth of having an all-around team of experts, quality products, market demand, strong customer commitment and — an eCommerce business plan.

Appendix A

BUSINESS PLAN
TABLE OF CONTENTS EXAMPLE

TABLE OF CONTENTS

2. Advisory Board
3. Strategic Alliances
4. Staff
5. Organization Structure

VI.   **OPERATIONS**
1. Strategy
2. Integrating eCommerce
3. Teams
4. Firewalls

VII.   **BUSINESS LOCATION AND EQUIPMENT**
1. Site and Facility Description
2. Suitability to the Business
3. Contractual Agreements
4. Equipment Description

VIII.   **FINANCIAL PLAN**
1. Risk Evaluation
2. Investment Proposal
3. Exit Strategy
4. Break-Even Analysis
5. Financial Projections
   • Five-Year Profit & Loss
   • Five-Year Cash Flow
   • Five-Year Balance Sheet
   • 12-Month Profit & Loss (if applicable)
   • 12-Month Cash Flow (if applicable)
6. Historical Financials (for existing companies)

LIST OF FIGURES
List figures in numerical order followed by the title

APPENDICES
Begin with Appendix A followed by the title

Appendix B

CONFIDENTIAL
BUSINESS PLAN SUMMARY

Reducing your business plan to a separate one-page summary is ideal for finding potential investors or providing business associates, bankers, and managers with a quick reference. An example is provided on the following page.

Nytec Corporation
Confidential Business Plan Summary
(Sample Text)

Business Description: NyTec is a software packaging closure manufacturer operating in both a virtual and traditional environment under the brand names of Easy Close and the patented Sure Lock with gross annual sales of $xx million. Targeting four market segments in the USA, Europe, Asia, and Australia, the company creates custom packaging that uses the closures. From the company's Website, clients are able to approve of their custom packaging from anywhere in the world and place orders over a secure network.

Background: NyTec is the outgrowth of a concept conceived and funded with $xx in 1989 by the company's founder and incorporated in 1992 with xxx authorized shares. There are xxx shares issued, xx percent owned by the founder. Having developed its product line and market, NyTec is now seeking second phase funding of $xx million in return for xx percent equity and one board seat. Based upon current projections, this represents xx percent ROI over a 36-month period plus equity in the company.

Management and Boards: The company's five key executives, with a combined 134 years experience, are highly regarded leaders in their respective fields. This management team is further enhanced by a highly qualified and accomplished advisory board who specialize in the software and packaging industries. Each of these six professionals has a minimum of ten years experience in their respective fields.

Strategic Alliances: NyTec has two strong strategic alliances. ABC, Ltd. adds both technology and marketing support to the company's long-term plans. Overseas Planner is a major group responsible for successfully launching popular software packages in foreign markets. NyTec licenses its products to Overseas for an annual fee as well as a xx percent share in gross profits.

Five-Year Sales Projections
($millions)

Years	Gross Sales	Net Before Taxes
1	$xx	$xx
2	xx	xx
3	xx	xx
4	xx	xx
5	xx	xx

Copies of this Business Plan are available upon request. Please contact:

(contact information here)

Worksheets

These worksheets are for personal use only.

Business Plan Scheme Sheet

WORKSHEET 1: Business Description

Business Description: _____

_____

_____

_____

_____

_____

_____

_____

Goals: _____

_____

_____

_____

_____

_____

_____

_____

Mission Statement: _____

_____

_____

_____

_____

_____

_____

_____

WORKSHEET 2: Executive Summary

As plan is developed, add major points.

_____

_____

_____

_____

_____

_____

_____

_____

_____

_____

_____

_____

_____

_____

_____

_____

_____

_____

_____

_____

_____

_____

_____

_____

_____

WORKSHEET 3: Business Information

My Enterprise: .com _____ .edu _____ . gov _____ .org. _____ other _____

Number of Employees: _____

_____

Number of Locations: _____

_____

_____

Website: Yes _____ No _____ Planning for one _____

_____

Internet Service Provider: _____

Address: _____

_____

Phone: _____

Email: _____

My URL: _____

Need Email: _____

Filter/Security Software: Yes _____ No _____ $ Range _____

What's Blocked: _____

_____

_____

_____

Who's Blocked:_____

_____

_____

_____

WORKSHEET 4: Description and Benefit

Description: _____

_____

_____

_____

_____

_____

_____

_____

_____

_____

_____

_____

Customer Benefits: _____

_____

_____

_____

_____

_____

_____

_____

_____

_____

_____

_____

WORKSHEET 5: Product Mix by Ratio to Sales

| | Percent of Sales | | | | | |
Product Mix	Past Performance		Projected			

WORKSHEET 6: Industry Growth

Past	5 Years	% Growth	Projected	5 Years	% Growth
19___	$_____	_____ %	_____	$_____	_____ %
19___	$_____	_____ %	_____	$_____	_____ %
19___	$_____	_____ %	_____	$_____	_____ %
19___	$_____	_____ %	_____	$_____	_____ %
19___	$_____	_____ %	_____	$_____	_____ %

Notes: _____

_____

_____

_____

_____

_____

_____

_____

_____

_____

_____

_____

_____

_____

_____

_____

WORKSHEET 7: Industry Overview

My Industry: _____ **SIC:** _____

Product Line: _____ **Sub-SIC:** _____

a. Major Assets	1.	_____
	2.	_____
	3.	_____
	4.	_____
b. Liabilities	1.	_____
	2.	_____
	3.	_____
	4.	_____

Major Marketing Regions

_____

_____

_____

Industry (major points, strengths, general comments):

_____

_____

_____

Notes: _____

_____

_____

_____

_____

WORKSHEET 8: Emerging Trends

Emerging Trends	Major Trend	Use of Application	Secondary Trend
User preferences:			
User demographics:			
New technologies:			
New markets:			
Labor:			
Communication:			
Internet:			

Notes: _____

_____

_____

_____

_____

WORKSHEET 9: User/Buyer Characteristics

User/Buyer Type	Percent have Website	$ Median Annual Expenditures	Rate of Consumption

WORKSHEET 10: Consumer/Buyer Profile*

Age	% of Market	Race	% of Market	Gender	% of Market
_____	_____%	Asian:		Female	_____%
_____	_____%	_____	_____%	Male	_____%
_____	_____%	_____	_____%	**Education**	
_____	_____%	Black:		Less than 12 yrs _____%	
_____	_____%	_____	_____%	Some college _____%	
_____	_____%	Caucasian:		2-yr. college _____%	
_____	_____%	_____	_____%	4-yr. college _____%	
_____	_____%	Hispanic:		Masters _____%	
_____	_____%	_____	_____%	Ph.D. _____%	
_____	_____%	American Indian:		**Income**	
_____	_____%	_____	_____%	$_____ to _____%	
_____	_____%	Other		$_____ to _____%	
_____	_____%	_____	_____%	$_____ to _____%	
_____	_____%	_____	_____%	$_____ to _____%	

Notes: _____

_____

_____

_____

_____

_____

* Regional data will vary. If pertinent, breakout differences by regions.

WORKSHEET 11: Industry Pricing Trends

Product*	Past Industry Pricing Trends			% Rate of Inflation for Same Period		
	19__	20__	20__	19__	20__	20__
_____	$____	$____	$____	____%	____%	____%
_____	$____	$____	$____	____%	____%	____%
_____	$____	$____	$____	____%	____%	____%
_____	$____	$____	$____	____%	____%	____%
_____	$____	$____	$____	____%	____%	____%
_____	$____	$____	$____	____%	____%	____%

Notes: _____

_____

_____

_____

_____

_____

_____

_____

_____

_____

* Describe by product mix.

WORKSHEET 12: Customer Service

Your Current Services	Standard Industry Practices	Emerging Trends	Your New Services

Notes: _____

WORKSHEET 13: Supplier Characteristics

Disadvantages   **Probable Solutions**

_____

_____

_____

Advantages   **Value Added**

_____

_____

_____

Notes: _____

_____

_____

_____

_____

WORKSHEET 14: Competition

Competitors	Annual Sales	Sales Tactics	On Yes	Web No	% Market Share
1._____	$_____	_____	_____	_____	_____%
2._____	$_____	_____	_____	_____	_____%
3._____	$_____	_____	_____	_____	_____%
4._____	$_____	_____	_____	_____	_____%
5._____	$_____	_____	_____	_____	_____%
6._____	$_____	_____	_____	_____	_____%
7._____	$_____	_____	_____	_____	_____%
8._____	$_____	_____	_____	_____	_____%

Notes: _____

_____

_____

_____

_____

_____

_____

_____

_____

_____

_____

WORKSHEET 15: Market Segments

| | Product Mix | | | |
Market Segment — Niche	I	II	III	IV

Notes: _____

_____

_____

_____

_____

_____

_____

_____

_____

_____

_____

WORKSHEET 16: Extranet and Intranet

	No. Pgs.	Internal No. Users	External No. Users

Extranet: Customer

_____

_____

_____

_____

_____

Extranet: Suppliers

_____

_____

_____

_____

_____

Intranet

_____

_____

_____

_____

_____

WORKSHEET 17: Website Content

Content	Phases* I II III	Firewall Yes No	Developmental Ideas and Comments

Extranet: Customer
User Instructions
Warranty Registration
Product Warranties

Extranet: Suppliers
Price Lists
Price Changes
Schematics

Intranet
Team Projects
   and Updates
Employee Training
Policies Manual
Marketing Research
Marketing Surveys

Public Access
Events and Demos
Company Background
Annual Report
Co. Email/Tel Directory
Employee Vita and Photo
Job Openings
Newsletter
Customer Services
Single Product Flyers
Catalog with 15 Products
Order Forms
Media Releases

*Determine Phase Timelines: Phase I: _____ Phase II: _____ Phase III: _____

WORKSHEET 18: Distribution Channels

Sales Unit	Distribution Channels	End-User and/or _____
	Can include Website marketing activities	

_____

_____

_____

_____

_____

_____

_____

_____

_____

_____

_____

_____

_____

_____

Notes: _____

_____

_____

_____

_____

WORKSHEET 19: Pricing Policies

Pricing Tier   **Description**

1. _____   _____
                      _____

2. _____   _____
                      _____

3. _____   _____
                      _____

4. _____   _____
                      _____

5. _____   _____
                      _____

6. _____   _____
                      _____

7. _____   _____
                      _____

8. _____   _____
                      _____

Notes: _____

_____

_____

_____

_____

WORKSHEET 20: Five-Year Sales Projections

Product Mix	Year	Annual Gross $	# Existing Accounts	# New Accounts	Projected Annual Gross
	1				
	2				
	3				
	4				
	5				
	1				
	2				
	3				
	4				
	5				
	1				
	2				
	3				
	4				
	5				

	Yr. 1	Yr. 2	Yr. 3	Yr. 4	Yr. 5
Combined Annual Gross					
Number of Employees					

WORKSHEET 21: Integrated Tactical Marketing Path

_____ **Tactical Marketing Path Activities**

(Use one worksheet for each tactic.)

Tactical Title:

Contact Team and Numbers:

Objectives:

Tactic:

Market Segment for This Package:

Three Client-Buying Considerations:

Competitors' Use of This Tactic:

Obstacles to This Tactic:

WORKSHEET 21: Integrated Tactical Marketing Path, continued

Action Plan	Timeline	Deadline	Persons
1.			
2.			
3.			
4.			
5.			
6.			
7.			
8.			

Success Milestones

Immediate: _____

6 Months: _____

12 Months: _____

Action	Costs*	No. of Hours	Action	Costs	No. of Hours
1.					
2.					
3.					

12-Month Use Frequency

Month

Jan	Feb	Mar	Apr	May	Jun	Jul	Aug	Sep	Oct	Nov	Dec

Weeks

1234	1234	1234	1234	1234	1234	1234	1234	1234	1234	1234	1234

Comments: _____

_____

Total Hours: _____   **Completion Date:** _____

Total Budget: _____   **Team Leader:** _____

* Estimate costs based on the following: Annual salary, plus benefits, times 15 percent G&A = Cost

WORKSHEET 22: **Media Planning**

Step 1: Review your sales projections.

Step 2: What media will you need to reach this market?

Step 3: What percentage of gross annual sales will be allocated to advertising?

Total budget: $_____

1. Newspapers   Y__   N__

2. Magazines   Y__   N__

3. TV   Y__   N__

4. Radio   Y__   N__

5. Direct Mail   Y__   N__

6. Billboards   Y__   N__

7. Bench signs   Y__   N__

8. Transportation signs   Y__   N__

     Taxis ___

     Buses ___

     Air Transports ___

     Subways ___

     Websites _____

     Directories _____

     Other _____

Step 4: Research the media you have selected for price, circulation, and reader demographics. Call the publication's advertising department and request advertising rate cards. Compile these findings on Worksheet 23: Media Selection.

Notes: _____

_____

_____

_____

_____

_____

WORKSHEET 23: Media Selection

Media Resource	Description of Advertising	Frequency	Cost per Ad	Total Cost

WORKSHEET 24: Related Ad Costs

Media	Graphic Design or Production Costs	Pre-print Costs	Postage and Printing	Other Costs

Notes: _____

WORKSHEET 25: 12-Month Advertising Schedule and Budget

Media Source and Description	Months J	F	M	A	M	J	J	A	S	O	N	D	Other Costs	Total

Annual Combined Total $ _____ $ _____

WORKSHEET 26: **Public Relations Ideas**

Budget: _____

Step 1: Highlight ideas for PR plan.

_____

_____

_____

_____

_____

_____

_____

_____

Step 2: Highlight PR theme.

_____

_____

_____

_____

_____

_____

_____

_____

WORKSHEET 27: Public Relations Activities

What (Media or Activity)	When (Dates)	Where (Location)	Who (Person Responsible)	Costs (Expenses and Time)

WORKSHEET 28: 12-Month Public Relations Schedule and Budget

Media Source and Description	Months J	F	M	A	M	J	J	A	S	O	N	D	Other Costs	Total

Annual Combined Total $_____ $_____

WORKSHEET 29: Management Team

**Executive
Name and Title**   **Describe Position** (Describe in three sentences or less)

_____

_____

_____

_____

_____

_____

_____

_____

_____

_____

_____

_____

_____

_____

_____

_____

_____

_____

_____

WORKSHEET 30: Advisory Board

Advisory
Name and Title   **Describe Position** (Describe in three sentences or less)

_____

_____

_____

_____

_____

_____

_____

_____

_____

_____

_____

_____

_____

_____

_____

_____

_____

_____

_____

_____

_____

_____

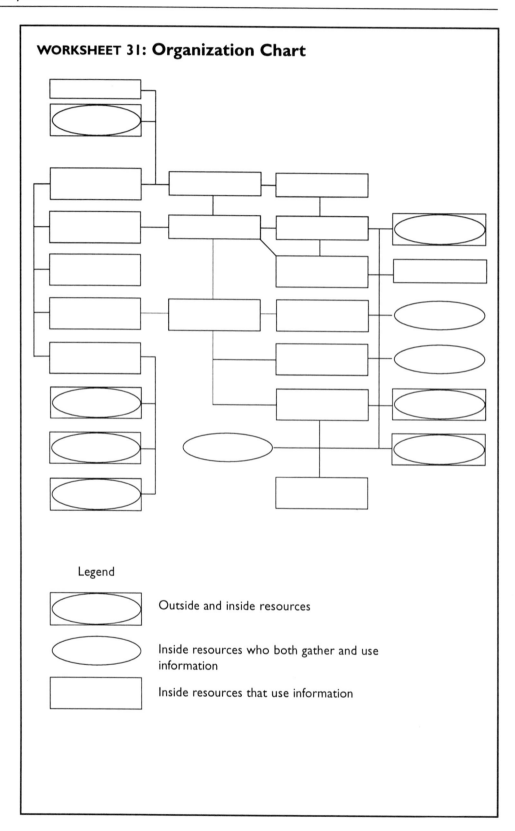

WORKSHEET 31: Organization Chart

Legend

Outside and inside resources

Inside resources who both gather and use information

Inside resources that use information

WORKSHEET 32: Operating Strategies

Group, Dept., Key Word, or Associates	Strategy	Results

* In addition to employees, the list might include strategic alliances or advisory board members who are paid to render specific services, such as a fulfillment house, contract manufacturer — an outsource of any kind.

WORKSHEET 33: Website Design

Name: _____

http: _____

Welcome to

Notes: _____

_____

_____

_____

_____

WORKSHEET 34: Merchant's Account

Merchant's Credit Bank Comparison (Bank Name and Contact Numbers)	Set-Up Costs	Rates	Comments

Notes: _____

WORKSHEET 35: Intranet Activity Planner

12-Month Training and Meeting Plan

Month	Week 1	Week 2	Week 3	Week 4	Notes
Jan					
Feb					
Mar					
Apr					
May					
Jun					
Jul					
Aug					
Sep					
Oct					
Nov					
Dec					

WORKSHEET 36: Firewalls

Risk Assessment*	Needs Analysis**	Software and Hardware	Cost

Notes: _____

_____

_____

_____

_____

* How much is your security worth?

** Define the kind of access an authorized outside user needs and vice versa.

WORKSHEET 37: Business Location

Site and facility: _____

_____

_____

_____

Suitability to the business: _____

_____

_____

_____

Contracts: _____

_____

_____

_____

Equipment/Existing: _____

_____

_____

_____

Equipment/Purchase: _____

_____

_____

_____

Glossary

ACH: Automatic Clearing House.

Address: A group of letters or numbers that give you an Internet identification.

AFK: Net jargon meaning, "Away from keyboard."

Anonymous FTP Servers: A computer with a large capacity to store a "data warehouse" of information, source codes, and graphics. Users find their way to the server, and with certain commands, transfer the information to their own computer.

Application Service Provider (APS): Your provider's host website where they will let you use as much or as little of their technology and software. A plus for small businesses.

Archie: A name derived from the word "archive," is a program on the Internet that helps with searches.

ASCII: American Standard Code for Information Interchange. ASCII has become a world standard for character code. Since ASCII characters are easy to transfer over the Internet, most email systems have used the ASCII format.

ASIC: Application Specific Integrated Circuits.

ASP: Application Service Provider.

Assumptions: An explanation of how line items are determined in financial projections. Also referred to as "Notes to Financials" or "Financial Footnotes."

Balance Sheet: A financial statement that shows the company's Assets and Liabilities.

Banner Ad: A display advertisement on Websites. Some are animated and in many instances will hot link to the advertiser's site when users click on the ad.

BBS: Bulletin Board System. Online services are large BBSs.

Benchmark: The best. Number one. A proven role model of excellence in a given area of business activity.

Bitnet: Begun in 1981 and operated by EDUCOM, Bitnet is a research and academic network meaning "Because It's Time Network."

Bookmark: A software function that allows you to maintain an electronic list of your favorite Websites. To return to the site by opening the bookmark and clicking on the name.

BRB: Net jargon meaning, "Be right back."

Break-Even: The point where a company's total sales equal total cost.

Browser: Software that allows you to search and navigate the Web. There are quite a few on the market. Some are better known than others, such as, Netscape Navigator.

Cache: An area in a computer's memory that makes it easy to retrieve stored data.

Campaign: An activity within an organization that produces a predetermined result within a specified time frame, e.g., advertising campaign, promotional campaign, fund-raising campaign, public relations campaign.

Capital: Money or property owned or used by a company. The total face value of a company's stock.

Cash Flow: Money or the equivalent paid to a company. Cash flow statements are usually estimated month-to-month although daily cash flow can be recorded as well.

CERN: The European High-Energy Particle Physics Lab in Geneva that developed the World Wide Web in 1991.

CDMA: Code Division Multiple Access technology serves as the basis for a new generation of digital wireless products and services developed by Qualcomm.

CIX: Commercial Internet Exchange. The NSF imposed an "acceptable use policy" restricting commerce on the Internet. This led organizations wanting to use the Net for commercial purposes to form CIX. CIX created an exchange point where providers of networking services could connect to each other without using the NSF backbone. NSF restrictions ended April 1995.

CGI: Common Gateway Interface. CGI scripts (or programming) are currently needed to make order forms work over the Internet.

Clueless Newbie: Someone new to the Internet who doesn't know his or her netiquette.

Coach: Coaching is a business moniker or nickname for boss or outside consultant. Delivery style, however, differs considerably.

Commercial Accounts: Business accounts at a bank or other financial institution.

Commercial Banks and Bankers: Those who cater to commercial accounts.

CISC: Complex Instruction Set Computer. A chip within a computer that supports as many as 200 instructions.

Cookies: Small pieces of code that are stored on your computer which let Webmasters track your activities on their Website.

Crash: When a computer system freezes (crashes) it is impossible to use.

Customer Service Resource (CSR): Live customer service contact over the Internet.

CTIA: Cellular Telephone Industry Association.

Cyberspace: A coined term used to loosely describe the global computer network. These computers are all connected to each other, making the Internet possible.

Database: A computerized format of information, such as, a suppliers' catalog and price lists, a collection of sales information, marketing demographics, etc.

DBS: Direct Broadcast Satellite.

Debt Financing: Money that is borrowed and must be repaid according to a contractual agreement between borrower and lender.

Distribution Channel: A sequential order in which goods and services travel from the producer to the end-user.

DNS: Domain Name Server

Domain Name: Like telephone numbers, domain names are a string of individualized words/letters helping computers in cyberspace connect users with their destination on the Web or to an email address.

Download: To transfer information from one computer in a remote location to another computer — usually your local computer. You do this each time you download your email or print out something from the Web.

Downsize: To reduce the overall size of a company; to cut expenses. This can mean a reduction in the number of employees, product lines or products offered and, facilities, in order to create a more profitable business. Over time, organizations get top heavy, making it all but impossible to avoid downsizing if they want to maintain a fresh spontaneity, steady growth and profitability.

DPI: Dots per square inch.

DVD: Digital Video Disc or Digital Versatile Disc. Discs are technically superior to CDs, CD-ROMs and VCR tapes. Hardware must be upgraded and/or changed to accommodate DVD.

eBusiness: A company conducting business on the Web.

eCommerce: Doing business electronically; a catch-word for conducting business on the Web.

Email: Electronic Mail that is transmitted over the Internet using your computer and a modem.

Encryption: Coding that creates privacy for sensitive information.

End-User: The last person who buys a product or service in the distributional chain; usually purchased for self-use, whether a company or individual.

Equity: Debt-free ownership of property. In business, investors buy an equity position or make and equity investment in a company forming a partnership-type of arrangement in exchange for their money.

Executive Premiums: Products which are sold to companies that, in turn, distribute them free to customers with whom they do business. These impersonal gifts, although not always, range in price between $5 and $20, such as, a business card case with or without the person's name on it.

Exit Advertising: A catch-phrase coined by Blender, a CD-ROM based company. Exit advertising forces Net readers to view at least five seconds of an ad between articles.

Exit Strategy: A proposed way for company founders and investors to dissolve their association with each other.

Firewall: A combination of software and hardware that isolates computers while permitting one-way connections.

Fixed Costs: Expenses that do not change. A loan payment would be a fixed amount whereas the utility bills would be different each month — variable costs.

Flame: A hostile email pointing out your wrong doing. You don't want one!

Freeware or Freenet: Not to be confused with shareware. This is software downloaded free over the Internet. Developers keep the master copy and some charge after a trial run; others offer a "lite" version of their software to sample prior to purchasing. Some very good software is offered free.

FTP: File Transfer Protocol. Handles remote directory listings and file transfers on the Internet.

GIF: Graphic Interchange Format. GIF is an image file format and is used on the World Wide Web.

Global Internet Project: … "is an international group of senior executives committed to spurring the growth of the Internet worldwide. The nonprofit group believes that the Internet must be viewed as a global medium transcending geographical differences … and is concerned about the Internet facing a growing maze of national laws … that may impede its growth." *www.gip.org/*

Goodwill: A public's respect for and good feeling about a company. Creating good will among potential customers or clients helps companies develop brand loyalty as well as sell their products and services.

Gopher: Gopher is a client/server application for indexing and retrieving information on the Internet. It is the predecessor to the World Wide Web. There is still a lot of important information available using Gopher. See Gopher Jewels list at: http://galaxy.einet.net/GJ/

Graphic: An artistic presentation where text and illustrations (photos included) are balanced to complete a display of information.

Home Page: An introductory screen on a Website.

Hot Link: A connection made between Webpages that make it easy to jump from one page to another with a point and click of the mouse.

HTML: Hypertext Markup Language. HTML is a code language versus a program language. It works in much the same way that word processor software works. It cannot create graphics.

http: Hypertext Transfer Protocol. http is the communication protocol used by all Web documents. When you type "http" at the beginning of an Internet address, you are telling your browser you want to go to the World Wide Web.

IAHC: See International Ad Hoc Committee.

ICP: Internet Content Provider. A company or individual providing Internet content to ISPs and others including their own Internet site.

Income Statement: Also referred to as the Profit and Loss Statement. It is a financial statement that details all of a company's income and expenses. When the expenses are subtracted from income, there will be a profit or loss.

Industrial Accounts: A market segment. Industrial accounts almost always refer to manufacturing companies.

Institutional Accounts: A market segment what includes hospitals, schools (all types), governments and other similar organizations.

Interest: A percentage earned on a principle sum of money.

International Ad Hoc Committee: A group of 11 representative organizations consisting of Internet, legal and other international standards groups that oversee the Internet. IAHC is the predecessor to the Policy Oversight Committee.

Internaut: Someone who uses the Internet regularly.

Internet: A global collection of computers networked together via a common protocol.

InterNIC: The InterNIC has been the sole source for registering domain names used on the Internet. The InterNIC is operated by Network Solutions, Inc., owned by SAIC (Science Applications International Corporation) and supported by the National Science Foundation. It is sometimes referred to as the NIC.

IP Address: All servers require an IP (Internet Protocol) address. To get one, send email to: Hostmaster@INTERNIC.NET or see InterNIC's Website at: http://rs.internic.net/rs-internic.html

Internet Access Provider: Also referred to as an Internet Service Provider or ISP.

Interstitials: A buzz-word used to describe a potential alternative to the banner ad on the Internet. It is used to catch the readers attention en route between Web pages. Its advantage to an advertiser is that it cannot be easily ignored.

Intranet: An internal Internet site accessible only to (all or certain) employees and designated users.

Inventory: Also referred to as stock in the retail trade. Inventory can be tangible or intangible. It is the excess a company has that is ready to be consumed in some way or sold.

IPO: Initial Public Offering.

IPP: Internet Presence Provider. A virtual marketing and consulting company that offers Web and Internet development services plus other assistance.

IRC: Internet Relay Chat. Using their keyboard, people can "talk" to each other in real-time over the Internet.

ISDN: Integrated Services Digital Network. Offered by most ISPs and used by many businesses, ISDN lines offer faster access to the Internet.

ISO9000: A globally recognized certificate of quality. An organization must meet certain criteria. There are a number of different certificates in the ISO9000 series.

ISP (Internet Service Provider): A telecommunications company which connects you to the Internet. They provide a local toll free number, software, and other services.

Line A: Group of products or services that make up what an organization offers for sale.

Line Item: Each line of type on a page is in a sequential order whether it is visually numbered or not. An item or issue on a certain line is a line item.

Lurk: To silently read and observe a newsgroup without posting messages or chatting.

Lynx: A text-based browser (software) that lets UNIX and VMS users navigate the Web by typing in digits that correspond to hypertext links. In so doing, the Web can be viewed as text only versus graphics and text.

Mailbox: A term used to describe where your email is stored on a server (computer).

Market: The physical attributes of where a company sells its wares.

Market Niche: A select and very focused market segment.

Market Potential: A product or service having met all the criteria demanded by customers or clients.

Market Saturation: There are too many of the same kind of products on the market and not enough buyers to absorb all of them. This usually happens a number of years (between 2 to 10 years) after a product has been introduced to the marketplace. Market saturation is a natural part of the product life cycle.

Market Size: The overall size of a market. For instance, a children's clothing retailer cannot sell to everyone living within its market because its products are only suited to children. Therefore, the retailer's market size is the number of children living within its marketing area whose ages are appropriate to the sizes of garments it sells.

Marketing Path: A highly detailed marketing and operational strategy for reaching projected levels of sales.

Mean: A middle point between extremes.

Media: All forms of communication, such as, print, TV, radio, signage, the Internet, etc.

Milestone: A significant point in the development of a project.

Modem: Think of a modem as a telephone with software. It allows your computer to communicate with another computer over phone lines and/or via satellite.

NCSA: National Computer Security Association (refer to Section VI. Quick Links).

Netiquette: A socially accepted etiquette (behavior) one uses on the Internet.

Network: A group of computers, usually in-company, that use the same protocol to exchange information.

Newsgroups: Groups of people on the Internet who share information about a specific topic. They "chat" online or post messages to each other. There are approximately 25,000 groups each with a special interest. If you don't want flamed don't post information outside the interest of the group or past advertising.

NSF: National Science Foundation. A U.S. Government funded organization responsible for the Internet backbone from 1969 through April 1995. The reality of the Internet today is that there is no single backbone. Instead there are multiple exchange points.

Outernet: Not on the Internet. The real world.

Operations: An overall approach or system for operating the many diverse aspects of an organization.

Organization Progression: As an organization grows, its structure will change. New departments will most likely be added as well as new managers and personnel. These are time-sequenced in the planning stages.

Passive Advertising: Advertising that keeps a company's name before the buying public, but does not prompt immediate action.

Payware: Upgrading and paying for Freeware.

Policy Oversight Committee: A group of companies to oversee the Internet. See Internet Ad Hoc Committee.

Points: A percentage of the loan amount that is paid up front as a fee for processing the loan.

Posting: Writing a message that is sent or left on the Internet.

PPP: Point-to-Point Protocol. A newer method of protocol that works like SLIP. It requires special software.

Profit and Loss: See Income Statement.

Promotion: A marketing activity that covers a broad range of selling tools. The store promoted its opening with clowns and balloons. They advertised the promotion. Some manufacturers helped the store by offering special co-op advertising discounts while others offered a wholesale discount of 25 percent opening day.

Public Relations: Another marketing activity that covers a broad spectrum of disciplines. In over simplified terms, public relations, like promotions, supports a company's marketing objectives in addition to creating its own agenda for helping the company develop good relations with its public.

Publicity: A highly desired form of free advertising — or free media exposure. "Advertising," according to one business proverb, "is what you pay for. Publicity is what you pray for."

Protocol: A common language that computers worldwide use to talk with each other. For example, TCP/IP.

R&D: Research and Development. Firms research and then develop their products or services.

Real Time: Online communication that allows users to chat with each other as if they were in the same room versus posting an email and waiting for a response.

Retail Banks: Banks that cater to the general public.

Risk: Refers to the possibility of financial loss. The investor's money was at risk — risk capital.

RISC: Reduced Instruction Set Computer. A computer architecture that has only a few instructions and performs them very fast.

R.O.I.: Return On Investment. Most investors want to see 10 times the return on their investment within five years.

ROM: Read only memory.

Sales Path: A distribution channel. How goods or services change hands to reach the end-user.

Search Engine: An Internet "tool" that allows users to search the Web for data using relevant key words. Search Engines are also used on large Websites as well as Intranets.

SET: Secure Electronic Transaction.

Shareware: Software that is distributed through public domain channels. Authors sometimes, though not always, expect to be compensated. There are hundreds, even thousands, of shareware programs on the Internet.

Shopping Cart: A description for selecting and later buying items on the Web.

Shout: If you type in all CAPITAL letters on the Internet, you are "shouting" and considered quite rude.

SIPC: Simply Interactive Personal Computer.

SLIP: Serial Line Internet Protocol. A type of connection to the Internet.

Small Business: Most companies with less than 1,500 employees and less than $21.5 million in receipts. To obtain a copy of the size standards table contact the Small Business Administration.

Smiley: Keyboard symbols used to express emotion online. There are around 200 altogether.

:-$	Smiley banker
%-)	User has been staring at the computer screen for 15 hours straight!
:-@	User is screaming …
~~:-(	A Net flame
>:->	User made a really devilish remark
:-/	User is skeptical
>:-<	User is mad
:I	Hmmmmmmmmmmmm
:-D	User is laughing — at you!
:-!	User is whispering

SMPT: Simple Mail Protocol Transfer. This is how email is exchanged over the Internet.

Snail Mail: Regular postal mail.

Spamming: A "junk email" technique where a sender emails hundreds or thousands of unsolicited messages to newsgroup members. To fight spam check out *www.spam.abuse.net*.

Strategy: A methodically worked out plan of action used by businesses and non-profits alike.

Tactics: Using a combination of specific plans to produce sales. One tactic might be giving free demonstrations to a group who could potentially buy the product or service. Another tactic might be to regularly send free information to customers.

Takeout Financing: Financing that is disbursed in ratio to expenditures.

Teams (Teaming): Groups of employees with diverse disciplines who are assigned to a specific project.

TCP/IP: Transmission Control Protocol/Internet Protocol. A language that computers use to talk to each other.

Top Heavy: Too many managers and executives and not enough workers.

TLD: Top Level Domains (domain names on the Internet).

Turnover: (also referred to as churn) The length of time it takes to buy and then resell something either tangible or intangible. The company lost money because of its slow inventory turnover. Inventory churn was greater than expected for a very profitable year. Also refers to human resources. Employees seldom leave the company, accounting for a very low turnover.

UPS: Uninterruptible Power Supply.

Universal Resource Indicator (URI): Another resource for conducting eCommerce; similar to an URL.

URL: Universal Resource Locator. A unique string of letters and marks that provides an individual identity for reaching you on the Web.

Variable Costs: Expenses in a business that vary from month to month such as the telephone.

Venture Capital: Money that is invested in a speculative business venture.

Virtual Reality: An interactive computer software feature that has the feel of emulating real world activities on or offline.

VPN: Virtual Private Network.

WAIS: Wide Area Information Server. WAIS is a program for searching databases on the Internet using specific key words in a document.

Web Browser: A browser is another name for the computer software that provides access to the Internet World Wide Web (WWW) .

Webcasting: Webcasting is the transmission of video and audio to multiple viewers on the Internet at the same time in much the same way as television.

Webite: A person using the Web.

Webmaster: A person who manages and coordinates all Web content. Job description varies somewhat from company to company.

Websetter: The new media equivalent of a print media typesetter. A Websetter does not create content, rather he or she puts together the words, art and writing of others using HTML code.

Website: A digital collection of text, graphics, or photos displayed by the site's owner for the benefit of others on the Internet.

WISC: Wide Instruction Set Computer.

World Wide Web (WWW): A large network on the Internet that supports graphics, audio, video, and text.

WYSIWYG: What you see is what you get.

XML eXtensible Markup Language: XML lets you say what data means; "smart data" is powering the eCommerce boon.

Jargon Generator

Although we have been warned by any number of power gurus to limit industry jargon in business plans, a littérateur would not be worth her/his salt without throwing in at least one meaningless phrase. The Jargon Generator is guaranteed by its creator[1] to impress absolutely everyone when you have nothing to say.

But won't I be called to task, you say? As the Sweetwater, Texas school administrator points out, "No one will ever admit they don't know what you're talking about. In fact, they will accept you as a decisive thinker who possesses great ability to verbalize complex ideas."

1. integrated	1. management	1. outputs
2. total	2. organizational	2. flexibility
3. systematized	3. monitored	3. analysis
4. parallel	4. reciprocal	4. mobility
5. functional	5. logistical	5. factors
6. responsive	6. transitional	6. concept
7. synchronized	7. modular	7. capability
8. compatible	8. creative	8. guidelines
9. balanced	9. operational	9. contingencies

How to use the Jargon Generator: The first two columns consist of polysyllabic adjectives, and the third contains ambiguous nouns that defy strict definition. Merely take any three-digit number and apply each digit to the corresponding sequential column. A 3-4-4 would be *systematized reciprocal mobility*; 8-2-1 is *compatible organizational outputs*; and 1-5-9 becomes *integrated logistical contingencies*. Any one of these erudite and impressive phrases will establish your authority and expertise in no time on any subject.

---

[1] Anonymously developed by a Sweetwater, Texas high school district administrator.

Index

Let *SmartStart* pave your way through today's complex business environment.

You may be like more than 35 million other Americans – you dream of owning a business. In fact, there has never been a better time to start a small business. According to a recent research study by the Entrepreneurial Research Consortium, one out of three U.S. households has someone who is involved in a small business startup. With statistics like these, the odds seem to be in your favor... until you start dealing with the many regulations, laws, and financial requirements placed on 21st century business owners.

SmartStart Your (State*) **Business** goes a step beyond other business how-to books and provides you with:

◆ Each book is state specific, with information and resources that are unique. This gives you an advantage over other general business start-up books that have no way of providing current local information you will need;

◆ Quick reference to the most current mailing and Internet addresses and telephone numbers for the federal, state, local, and private agencies that will help get your business up and running;

◆ State population statistics, income and consumption rates, major industry trends, and overall business incentives to give you a better picture of doing business in your state; and

◆ Logical checklists, sample forms, and a complete sample business plan to assist you with the numerous start-up details.

SmartStart is your roadmap to avoid legal and financial pitfalls and direct you through the bureaucratic red tape that often entangles fledgling entrepreneurs. This is your all-in-one resource tool that will give you a jump start on planning for your business.

SmartStart Your (State*) **Business**
$19.95, paperback

* When ordering, be sure to tell us which state you are interested in receiving.

Order direct from The Oasis Press®

You can order any Successful Business Library title directly from The Oasis Press® We would be happy to hear from you and assist you in finding the right titles for your small business needs at:

1-800-228-2275

Because *SmartStart* is a new state-specific series, new states are being released every month, please call to confirm a state's scheduled release date — or check with your favorite bookstore.

The Oasis Press®
Home to The Successful Business Library

— 1-800-228-2275 —

International Calls +1.541.479.9464

http://www.psi-research.com/oasis

HOW TO ORDER

Mail: Send this completed order form and a check, money order or credit card information to: PSI Research/The Oasis Press®, P.O. Box 3727, Central Point, Oregon 97502-0032

Fax: Available 24 hours a day, 7 days a week at **1-541-245-6505**

Email: **info@psi-research.com** (Please include a phone number, should we need to contact you.)

Web: Purchase any of our products online at our Website at **http://www.psi-research.com/oasis/**

Inquiries and International Orders: Please call **1-541-245-6502**

Indicate the quantity and price of the titles you would like:

TITLE	BINDER ISBN	PAPER ISBN	BINDER	PAPERBACK	QTY.	TOTAL
Advertising Without An Agency		1-55571-429-3		☐ 19.95		
Before You Go Into Business Read This		1-55571-481-1		☐ 17.95		
Bottom Line Basics	1-55571-329-7 (B)	1-55571-330-0 (P)	☐ 39.95	☐ 19.95		
BusinessBasics		1-55571-430-7		☐ 16.95		
The Business Environmental Handbook	1-55571-304-1 (B)	1-55571-163-4 (P)	☐ 39.95	☐ 19.95		
Business Owner's Guide to Accounting and Bookkeeping		1-55571-381-5		☐ 19.95		
businessplan.com		1-55571-455-2		☐ 19.95		
Buyer's Guide to Business Insurance	1-55571-310-6 (B)	1-55571-162-6 (P)	☐ 39.95	☐ 19.95		
California Corporation Formation Package		1-55571-464-1 (P)		☐ 29.95		
Collection Techniques for a Small Business	1-55571-312-2 (B)	1-55571-171-5 (P)	☐ 39.95	☐ 19.95		
College Entrepreneur Handbook		1-55571-503-6		☐ 16.95		
A Company Policy & Personnel Workbook	1-55571-364-5 (B)	1-55571-486-2 (P)	☐ 49.95	☐ 29.95		
Company Relocation Handbook	1-55571-091-3 (B)	1-55571-092-1 (P)	☐ 39.95	☐ 19.95		
CompControl	1-55571-356-4 (B)	1-55571-355-6 (P)	☐ 39.95	☐ 19.95		
Complete Book of Business Forms		1-55571-107-3		☐ 19.95		
Connecting Online		1-55571-403-X		☐ 21.95		
Customer Engineering	1-55571-360-2 (B)	1-55571-359-9 (P)	☐ 39.95	☐ 19.95		
Delivering Legendary Customer Service		1-55571-520-6 (P)		☐ 14.95		
Develop and Market Your Creative Ideas		1-55571-383-1		☐ 15.95		
Developing International Markets		1-55571-433-1		☐ 19.95		
Doing Business in Russia		1-55571-375-0		☐ 19.95		
Draw the Line		1-55571-370-X		☐ 17.95		
The Essential Corporation Handbook		1-55571-342-4		☐ 21.95		
Essential Limited Liability Company Handbook	1-55571-362-9 (B)	1-55571-361-0 (P)	☐ 39.95	☐ 21.95		
Export Now	1-55571-192-8 (B)	1-55571-167-7 (P)	☐ 39.95	☐ 24.95		
Financial Decisionmaking		1-55571-435-8		☐ 19.95		
Financial Management Techniques	1-55571-116-2 (B)	1-55571-124-3 (P)	☐ 39.95	☐ 19.95		
Financing Your Small Business		1-55571-160-X		☐ 19.95		
Franchise Bible	1-55571-366-1 (B)	1-55571-526-5 (P)	☐ 39.95	☐ 27.95		
The Franchise Redbook		1-55571-484-6		☐ 34.95		
Friendship Marketing		1-55571-399-8		☐ 18.95		
Funding High-Tech Ventures		1-55571-405-6		☐ 21.95		
Home Business Made Easy		1-55571-428-5		☐ 19.95		
Improving Staff Productivity		1-55571-456-0		☐ 16.95		
Information Breakthrough		1-55571-413-7		☐ 22.95		
Insider's Guide to Small Business Loans		1-55571-488-9		☐ 19.95		
Keeping Score: An Inside Look at Sports Marketing		1-55571-377-7		☐ 18.95		
Kick Ass Success		1-55571-518-4		☐ 18.95		
Know Your Market	1-55571-341-6 (B)	1-55571-333-5 (P)	☐ 39.95	☐ 19.95		
Leader's Guide: 15 Essential Skills		1-55571-434-X		☐ 19.95		
Legal Expense Defense	1-55571-349-1 (B)	1-55571-348-3 (P)	☐ 39.95	☐ 19.95		
A Legal Road Map for Consultants		1-55571-460-9		☐ 18.95		
Location, Location, Location		1-55571-376-9		☐ 19.95		
Mail Order Legal Guide	1-55571-193-6 (B)	1-55571-190-1 (P)	☐ 45.00	☐ 29.95		
Managing People: A Practical Guide		1-55571-380-7		☐ 21.95		
Marketing for the New Millennium		1-55571-432-3		☐ 19.95		
Marketing Mastery	1-55571-358-0 (B)	1-55571-357-2 (P)	☐ 39.95	☐ 19.95		
Money Connection	1-55571-352-1 (B)	1-55571-351-3 (P)	☐ 39.95	☐ 24.95		
Moonlighting: Earning a Second Income at Home		1-55571-406-4		☐ 15.95		
Navigating the Marketplace: Growth Strategies for Small Business		1-55571-458-7		☐ 21.95		
No Money Down Financing for Franchising		1-55571-462-5		☐ 19.95		
Not Another Meeting!		1-55571-480-3		☐ 17.95		
People-Centered Profit Strategies		1-55571-517-6		☐ 18.95		

Sub-total for this side:

TITLE		ISBN	BINDER	PAPERBACK	QTY.	TOTAL
People Investment	1-55571-187-1 (B)	1-55571-161-8 (P)	☐ 39.95	☐ 19.95		
Power Marketing for Small Business		1-55571-524-9 (P)		☐ 19.95		
Proposal Development	1-55571-067-0 (B)	1-55571-431-5 (P)	☐ 39.95	☐ 21.95		
Prospecting for Gold		1-55571-483-8		☐ 14.95		
Public Relations Marketing		1-55571-459-5		☐ 19.95		
Raising Capital	1-55571-306-8 (B)	1-55571-305-X (P)	☐ 39.95	☐ 19.95		
Renaissance 2000		1-55571-412-9		☐ 22.95		
Retail in Detail		1-55571-371-8		☐ 15.95		
The Rule Book of Business Plans for Startups		1-55571-519-2		☐ 18.95		
Secrets of High Ticket Selling		1-55571-436-6		☐ 19.95		
Secrets to Buying and Selling a Business		1-55571-489-7		☐ 24.95		
Secure Your Future		1-55571-335-1		☐ 19.95		
Selling Services		1-55571-461-7		☐ 14.95		
SmartStart Your (State) Business		varies per state		☐ 19.95		
Indicate which state you prefer:						
Small Business Insider's Guide to Bankers		1-55571-400-5		☐ 18.95		
Start Your Business		1-55571-485-4		☐ 10.95		
Strategic Insights		1-55571-505-2		☐ 19.95		
Strategic Management for Small and Growing Firms		1-55571-465-X		☐ 24.95		
Successful Network Marketing		1-55571-350-5		☐ 15.95		
Surviving Success		1-55571-446-3		☐ 19.95		
TargetSmart!		1-55571-384-X		☐ 19.95		
Top Tax Saving Ideas for Today's Small Business		1-55571-463-3		☐ 16.95		
Truth About Teams		1-55571-482-X		☐ 18.95		
Twenty-One Sales in a Sale		1-55571-448-X		☐ 19.95		
WebWise	1-55571-501-X (B)	1-55571-479-X (P)	☐ 29.95	☐ 19.95		
What's It Worth?		1-55571-504-4		☐ 22.95		
Which Business?		1-55571-390-4		☐ 18.95		
Write Your Own Business Contracts	1-55571-196-0 (B)	1-55571-487-0 (P)	☐ 39.95	☐ 24.95		

Success Series	ISBN		PAPERBACK	QTY.	TOTAL
50 Ways to Get Promoted	1-55571-506-0		☐ 10.95		
You Can't Go Wrong By Doing It Right	1-55571-490-0		☐ 14.95		

Oasis Software	FORMAT	BINDER		QTY.	TOTAL
Company Policy Text Files CD-ROM	CD-ROM ☐		☐ 49.95		
Company Policy Text Files Book & CD-ROM Package	CD-ROM ☐	☐ 89.95 (B)	☐ 69.95 (P)		
Winning Business Plans in Color CD-ROM	CD-ROM ☐		☐ 59.95		

Subtotal from other side	
Subtotal from this side	
▶ Shipping	
TOTAL	

Ordered by: *Please give street address*

NAME _____ TITLE _____

COMPANY _____

STREET ADDRESS _____

CITY _____ STATE _____ ZIP _____

DAYTIME PHONE _____ EMAIL _____

Ship to: *If different than above*

NAME _____ TITLE _____

COMPANY _____

STREET ADDRESS _____

CITY _____ STATE _____ ZIP _____

DAYTIME PHONE _____

Shipping:

YOUR ORDER IS:	ADD:
0-25	5.00
25.01-50	6.00
50.01-100	7.00
100.01-175	9.00
175.01-250	13.00
250.01-500	18.00
500.01+	4% of total

PLEASE CALL FOR RUSH SERVICE OPTIONS.
INTERNATIONAL ORDERS, PLEASE CALL FOR A QUOTE ON CURRENT SHIPPING RATES.

Payment Method:

☐ CHECK   ☐ MONEY ORDER
☐ AMERICAN EXPRESS   ☐ DISCOVER
☐ MASTERCARD   ☐ VISA

CREDIT CARD NUMBER

EXPIRATION (MM/YY)   NAME ON CARD (PLEASE PRINT)

SIGNATURE OF CARDHOLDER (REQUIRED)

Fax this order form to: (541) 245-6505 or mail it to: P.O. Box 3727, Central Point, Oregon 97502
For more information about our products or to order online, visit http://www.psi-research.com

OASIS PRESS BOOKS & SOFTWARE

04172000